Your

to Citing & Using
History Sources

Sources provide *information,*
from which we
identify *evidence* for *analysis.*

A conclusion
drawn from sound analysis
may then stand as *proof.*

Your *Stripped Bare Guide* to Citing & Using History Sources

The Briefcase Edition of
Evidence Explained:
Citing History Sources from Artifacts to Cyberspace

Elizabeth Shown Mills

2025
Genealogical Publishing Company
Baltimore, Maryland

PRINT & E-LIBRARY EDITIONS PUBLISHED BY
Genealogical Publishing Company, Inc.
Baltimore, Maryland

ISBN 9780806321523

Cover art:
Based on Stripped Bare Professor by Peter Hesse

*C*ontents

Foreword 9

Part One: Fundamentals

Source Usage &
Evidence Analysis 15
Documentation 35

Part Two: Constructing Citations

Construction Basics...................... 61
Universal Templates 83

Appendixes

Glossary 107

Further Study........................... 121

Index 127

Figures

1. Guidelines for Analyzing Evidence 18

2. Guidelines for Documentation 36

3. Two Functions of a Source Note 39

4. Placement of Note Numbers 45

5. Abbreviation Tips 55

6. Stylistic Tips for Source Notes 56

7. Bibliographic Tips 57

In memory of
the mistakes I made,
the guesswork I put into the wild,
and the cringes I caused myself
before I took to heart
the basics in this little manual

*F*oreword

In 1980 Richard S. Lackey's *Cite Your Sources* was introduced by the University Press of Mississippi as the first citation guide that specifically targeted those who study historical documents. Its title quickly became a mantra for many. But in the years since, that catchy refrain—*cite your sources*—has, too often, morphed into *cite something.*

And so, Your Stripped Bare Caution No. 1: citing an unreliable source will produce unreliable results. Period.

Successful research is research that yields *correct* information. Achieving that requires a sound analysis of everything we use. Identifying our source (i.e., citing it) is fundamental. The validity of any piece of information cannot be determined if its source is unknown. Beyond this, the reliability of any piece of information we take from a source cannot be analyzed if the *nature* of the source is not known—whether it is an original document or a derivative work, whether it was created by a responsible official, and what circumstances influenced its creation.

Merely citing a source is not enough, because all sources are not created equal.

Research, analysis, and citation are all parts of the same process. Research is not a matter of looking up names. It is not a gathering of "facts." Research requires appraisal of every piece of information we find. It requires correlation of details within each document and across the spectrum of all we gather. It requires the mental processing of random information into sound evidence. None of this analysis is possible if we do not thoughtfully and completely identify the source of each piece of information.

Lackey's manual, as a standard guide for students of history and genealogy, was replaced in 1997 by my first, slim manual *Evidence! Citation & Analysis for the Family Historian.* In 2007 it was greatly expanded to more fully meet the needs of history researchers as technology and the Internet exploded the availability of historical materials. But the heft of that 2007 manual—*Evidence Explained: Citing History Sources from Artifacts to Cyberspace,* now in its fourth edition—is a bit intimidating for some new researchers.

Your Stripped Bare Guide to Citing & Using History Sources offers the best of both: the simplicity of the little *Evidence!* updated with *Evidence Explained's* critical instruction on the building of cita-tions—including its game-changing universal templates that enable even beginning researchers to cite any type of historic record, in any form, no matter how or where it is accessed.

Like the original *Evidence!, Your Stripped Bare Guide* tries to strip away the confusion that researchers experience at the start of their adventures. It offers a road map to help you avoid mistakes and guideposts to keep you safe as you explore new materials.

As you use this guide in the course of your daily work, please bear in mind three things:

- Effective source citation is an *art,* not a *science.* No formula can cover all situations that researchers encounter. If you understand the *reasons why* certain patterns are followed and certain steps are taken, you can devise sound citations of your own as circumstances require.

- After nearly three decades, the Evidence Style citations used in this manual have become the standard within some branches of history and the recommended style of many journals. However, publishers often have a traditional house style that strips citations to a bare minimum to curtail printing costs. When we submit material to any publication, we are expected to follow its preferred style.

- *Your Stripped Bare Guide,* like Evidence Explained and its *Quick-Sheets,* is designed for use at *input* (the point of data collection), not *output* (eventual publication). With any project, as our research expands, we find contradictions in our information or conclusions—contradictions that require us to reevaluate the evidence we have drawn from our sources. Evidence Style citations enable us to make evaluations from our working files, without having to relocate rare sources in now-inaccessible locales. Evidence Style citations include all the elements that major publishers require. By recording this data in our research notes during input, we will have all essentials from which eventual editors can fill their needs without repeated research on our part or theirs.

Above all, take this to heart: The purpose of source citations is not to create paranoia or anxiety. Documenting our work *eliminates* angst by preventing mistakes and misunderstandings. The Evidence Style citations used in *Your Stripped Bare Guide* will help you avoid roadblocks in your research journey by understanding (a) the nature of each source you use; and (b) the strengths and weaknesses of the information that each source provides.

Part One
Fundamentals

*F*undamentals of Source Usage & Evidence Analysis

People. *Where did they come from? When? Who produced them? What did they do? Why?*

These are the most basic questions that history researchers ask. They are also questions we must ask of our information. *Where did it come from? Who produced it?* History's *why* question also applies to the sources of our information in a critically important way: *Why should we believe it?*

Within the answers to these simple queries lies all justification for accepting or rejecting the information we uncover.

The fact that words are spoken or written does not make them *true.* The appearance of a name, date, place, or statement on a piece of paper or somewhere in cyberspace does not make the information *true.* Nor does its existence prove that any individual mentioned therein is the same-name person we seek.

The past we explore is a fascinating spiral of false leads, confused identities, and tangled lives. When we study history, our challenge is to unearth every relevant record and weigh every detail so carefully that we piece together *accurately* each event and each life.

All research fields have practices and standards. Core principles are often the same across diverse fields. Yet significant differences have also developed to meet the particular needs of each. Whatever our area of interest, to pursue it well we learn its methods and standards and apply them appropriately. They are our guardrails and our safety nets. If we follow them, we are far less likely to hit roadblocks and far more likely to achieve our research goals.

Historical research—reliably done—requires a critical approach to both information and knowledge. *Unless you are repeating research already done on major public figures, answers to your research questions will not be ones you can easily "look up" in library books or online databases.* If you do find ready-made answers to a research question, they will often contradict each other. If no conflict is apparent, they may still be wrong. The original documents that you seek are just as suspect; you will need to persistently question the motive and the knowledge of each record's creator.

Is this cynical? No, just cautious. As researchers, we do not speculate; we test. We critically observe and carefully record. Then we must weigh the accumulated evidence—analyzing the individual parts as well as the whole, without favoring any theory. Bias, ego, patronage, prejudice, pride, or shame cannot tinge our decisions when we appraise our evidence.

The reality of our work is this: historical "truth" is elusive. When we research society or events, we will find many conflicting opinions among prior writers. If our research is genealogical, we will find that, prior to genetic testing, legal proof of relationships was usually based on assumption and trust. Yet, all families have had situations in which someone's parentage has been debated. We cannot—a generation, a century, a half-millenium later—*prove* a fact or a relationship beyond any shadow of doubt. Not even with genetic testing.

Every "fact" we assert, every identity we establish, every kinship we propose is simply *a decision we make from the body of evidence we have accumulated.* Our challenge is to locate and examine all surviving records, to assemble the best evidence possible, and to train ourselves to analyze and interpret that evidence wisely.

To help you toward that goal, this chapter surveys thirteen basic guidelines that reliable researchers apply to the analysis of historical records.

1

Sources, information, evidence, **and** *proof* **are not synonymous terms.**

Sources provide *information,* from which we identify *evidence* for *analysis.* A conclusion drawn from sound analyses may then stand as *proof.* This blueprint serves all who pursue history.

In many fields that work with sources and records, all material is lumped into one of two broad groups—*primary* or *secondary*—and then accepted or questioned accordingly. Within this generalization:

- *Primary sources* are generally said to be those created at the time of an event (regardless of whether the creator had firsthand knowledge of the subject)—as well as documents that have been copied and processed in all kinds of formats (thereby introducing alterations, omissions, misinterpretations, misreadings, and other copying errors).

- *Secondary sources* would be all else.

Realistically, most historical materials defy a clear assignment to either generalization. Yesteryear's diarists related the gossip of their time and place—unfiltered and often sensationalized; privileging them as a primary source does not make them reliable. Historical newspapers regularly published "news" that later proved untrue. Official census takers collected information on families from neighbors

Stripped Bare Guide

| Figure 1 |

Guidelines for Analyzing Evidence

1. *Sources, information, evidence,* and *proof* are not synonymous terms.

2. Reliable historical conclusions are based on the *weight* of the evidence found—not the *amount* of information or the *number* of times a statement has been asserted by others.

3. Reliable proof requires information to be drawn from a variety of independently created sources.

4. Original source material usually is more reliable than derivatives, but any document can contain errors.

5. The reliability of a derivative work is influenced by the amount and type of processing it has undergone.

6. The purpose of a record and the motivation of its creators frequently affect its truthfulness.

7. The most reliable informants, as a rule, have firsthand knowledge of the events to which they testify.

8. The veracity and skill of a record's creator will have shaped its content.

9. Timeliness generally adds to a document's credibility.

10. Penmanship should be studied for clues to identities, dates, and authenticity.

11. A record's custodial history affects its trustworthiness.

12. All known records should be used and a thorough effort made to identify unknown materials.

13. The case is never closed on a historical or genealogical conclusion.

who did not have an accurate knowledge of the household members, their ages, their birthplaces, occupations, property ownership, literacy, or relationships to each other. Court cases, pension and claim files, and other official documents are rife with affidavits containing intentionally false statements.

For these reasons, the most careful students of history follow a more critical model: one that separates *sources* from the *information* found within those sources. Each element is then evaluated by three factors that significantly affect reliability.

Sources: Entities that provide information

Sources are the containers of information. They may be human, physical, or virtual. They are the people who tell us things. They are the articles, books, documents, gravestones, or *objets d'art* from which we gather information.

Sources come in three basic forms that broadly speak to reliability:

- *Original records:* those that exist exactly as they were created the first time they were put into a physical form.

- *Derivative materials*: abstracts, transcriptions, translations, databases, etc., that aim to make original documents (or their information) more accessible.

- *Narrative accounts*: a mix of quality in which authors use their own words to present their "new and original" conclusions, drawn from their work in (presumably) both original and derivative sources.

Information: Content contained within a source

The details we take from our sources—that is, their *information*—also come in three basic forms:

- *Primary information*, provided by someone with firsthand knowledge.

- *Secondary information*, provided by someone with secondhand (or even more remote) knowledge of the event.

- **Unknown status,** a situation occurring when the identity of the informant or the nature of their role in the event is undetermined.

Evidence: Information relevant to a specific research question

Evidence also comes in three basic types:

- **Direct evidence:** information that directly addresses our research question and points to an answer without the addition of details from elsewhere. Direct evidence may be correct or incorrect.

- **Indirect evidence:** relevant information that does not directly answer the research question but can be used with other evidence to build a case supporting our hypothesis.

- **Negative evidence:** a hypothesis drawn from *a significant silence in the records* that should not exist given the specific set of circumstances. Negative evidence should *not* be confused with two similar terms: a *negative search* (i.e., a search that did not yield anything relevant) or *negative findings* (findings that contradict our hypothesis).

Direct evidence is easier to understand, but indirect evidence can carry equal or more weight. To use indirect evidence effectively, we need to sharpen our analytical skills and grow our understanding of the strengths and limits of various source materials. To use negative evidence reliably, we must deeply study the *context* of the lives we are researching, as well as the records. Recognizing a significant *silence* in the records or in a person's actions requires us to understand, first, what is *normal* to the place, time, and circumstances.

2

Reliable historical conclusions are based on the *weight* of the evidence found—not the *amount* of information or the *number* of times a statement has been asserted by others.

Each time we accept or reject information, that decision should be based upon careful consideration of where the *weight* of the evidence lies. That weight lies within the *quality* of the evidence, not the number of documents accumulated—even though *reliable research requires us to identify and consult all relevant sources.* As we weigh our evidence critically, we often find factors that both support and discount the hypothesis we seek to prove. If we do not find contra-dictions, we should be doubly sure that we have not overlooked any relevant sources or research strategies.

Thorough research customarily results in one of three situations:

- *A simple accumulation of direct evidence:* We may uncover multiple pieces of evidence that directly state the information we need. If that evidence satisfies the other requirements discussed in this chapter, then we will prove our hypothesis by simply citing each piece of evidence that supports the conclusion.

- *An assembly of indirect evidence:* We may never find even one document that states explicitly what we need to know (i.e., direct evidence), although we may find multiple pieces of evidence that collectively suggest one particular answer, with no contradictions that cannot be resolved. If so, then we may build a case from our assembly of indirect evidence.

- *A resolution of conflicting evidence:* The body of evidence we ac-cumulate—direct, indirect, or negative—may conflict in its details. In these cases, we would weigh each piece for credibility, do addi-tional research as warranted, and eventually resolve the conflicts with sound reasoning and supporting evidence.

In no case can we reach a reliable decision from a single piece of evidence—even direct evidence—because errors abound in all types of records.

Building a case, when documents disagree or do not state directly what we want to know, requires us to understand how *evidence* (relevant information) becomes *proof* (information or argument that is sound enough to be accepted).

Many students of history are already familiar with words commonly used to describe *evidence*. We've absorbed them from legal thrillers, hit television shows, or the daily news. However, every field has its *significant differences designed to meet its particular needs.*

As students of history, for example, we are heavy users of legal documents, but our analyses and our decisions have their own language and practices. The pursuit of history requires a higher standard of proof than does most civil litigation. Consider these comparisons:

- *The justice system* requires that a date be set for trial, that all known and valid evidence be considered at this time, and that a decision be made then and there on the basis of that evidence. To keep the court system flowing smoothly, the law calls for decisions to be made even in the closest of cases—even when the evidence on one side barely outweighs that on the other. This is the legal standard of proof called *preponderance of the evidence.**

- *History students in an academic setting* also face arbitrary deadlines set by instructors who must evaluate their work before the end of a semester or before the granting of a degree. Under this pressure, the *preponderance of the evidence* principle might serve as a stopgap measure—recognizing that thorough research still remains to be done and that all issues should be resolved before those students offer their work for publication.

- *Mature researchers, both genealogists and practicing historians,* are held to a higher standard. If sound evidence does not exist to

---

* Another legal term that is sometimes used by laymen who venture into history—*clear and convincing evidence*—is also inappropriate for history research because even the legal field has not agreed on a common standard for "clear and convincing." Some jurisdictions equate it with *beyond a reasonable doubt* (the standard for criminal cases), while others treat it as an intermediate standard between "no reasonable doubt" and a simple "preponderance."

See Henry Campbell Black, *Black's Law Dictionary,* 12th ed., Bryan A. Garner, editor (Eagen, Minnesota: Thomson Reuters, 2024), terms: "beyond a reasonable doubt," "clear and convincing proof," and "preponderance of the evidence."

accept or reject a hypothesis, we are expected to simply delay a decision until sound evidence is found.

That "sound evidence" is well defined by the five criteria of the Genealogical Proof Standard (GPS):*

1. **Reasonably exhaustive research** using all available sources.

2. **Sound documentation** for every source, with conclusions based only on the best surviving sources.

3. **Correlation and analysis of evidence**—that is, analysis of individual details as well as analysis of the whole body of evidence.

4. **Resolution of any conflicting evidence.**

5. **Presentation of a written proof argument, proof summary, or proof statement** that identifies all resources as well as all reasoning.*

Regardless of the branch of history that we pursue, these five criteria allow us to judge the reliability of any conclusion we reach, any point we assert, or any proposition put forth by another researcher.

To restate the obvious, because it is routinely ignored: *no conclusion is justified if we have not yet met the first element of the GPS, reasonably exhaustive research.* Both during and after our research, we carefully analyze each source and each piece of information, applying at least the points set forth in this chapter (which develop Criteria 2 and 3). If the weight of the evidence suggests a reasonable conclusion, we should labor to disprove our hypothesis as diligently as we labor to prove it. When we find contrary evidence, we must adequately and logically rebut it—or else delay our decision until clearer support can be assembled (Criteria 4). When we are convinced that all valid evidence points to just one conclusion that we

---

* Academic history has not defined a similar gauge, but this genealogical standard is appropriate for all branches of history. For the GPS and the forms of written proof, see Board for Certification of Genealogists, *Genealogy Standards,* 2d ed, rev. (Nashville: Turner Publishing, Ancestry imprint, 2021).

and others of experience and rational thinking can accept, then we may be ready to address Criteria 5: presenting our case.

To argue a case, we must reduce our argument to paper. The objective is a clearly written, logically reasoned, totally documented summary of the problem, the records consulted, the methodology and strategies used, the evidence found, and the conclusion we believe is justified.

3

Reliable proof requires information to be drawn from a variety of independently created sources.

No one source provides *proof*. Reliability is not determined by memorizing a list of authors, sources, or source types that might be deemed "trustworthy" alongside a list of those that are not. No source or source type is beyond error. All sources are created by humans and all humans err.

Therefore, *proof* is based upon the *body of evidence* we assemble to support the assertion we are making.

Sometimes, it is argued simplistically that a point is "proved" only if we have *x-number* of sources that report the same fact—but there is no magic number. The crucial issues are these:

- the *nature* and *quality* of each individual source;
- the *origin* of the source's information; and
- the *thoroughness* with which we use all surviving materials.

If we fortuitously find more than one source that states a specific piece of information we need, then we must ask a question: *Are those sources independently created?* If fraudulent testimony is given in a court case in 1742, then a nineteenth-century writer reports the details of that case in a local history, and a modern historian repeats the account in a university-press monograph, we might say that we have three different sources stating the same "facts." Does that *prove* what is being asserted? No. We do not have three *independently created* sources that coincidentally verify one another. We have one bad piece of information that has been thoughtlessly perpetuated.

4

Original source material usually is more reliable than derivatives, but any document can contain errors.

The modern world delivers "records" in endless formats. In addition to the originals preserved in archives and libraries, records have been transcribed or translated, abstracted, and published in print and online media. Documents have been imaged with antiquated equipment that diminishes legibility—or they may have been enhanced to improve upon flaws within the original. Details from documents may be extracted into databases and indexes, with drastic differences in reliability.

As we learned under Guideline 1, an *original source* is the first recording of something—its first fixation into a physical, permanent means. However, both law and technology recognize one exception:

- **Duplicates:** As defined by *Federal Civil Judicial Procedure and Rules*, Rule 1001 (e)—otherwise known as the Best Evidence Rule—a duplicate "means a counterpart, produced by a mechanical, photographic, chemical, electronic, or other equivalent process or technique that accurately reproduces the original."[*]

  Rule 1003 of the same code addresses the acceptability of duplicates. In courts of law, under most circumstances, a duplicate is

---

[*] *Federal Civil Judicial Procedure and Rules* (Eagan, Minnesota: The West Group, 2024), 452.

as admissible as the original would be. However, the presenter of a duplicate is obligated to explain why it is presented in lieu of the original. The history researcher has this same obligation.

Duplicates are a staple of historical research. Official and business correspondence prior to the mid-twentieth century used letter-press and carbon processes to produce file copies. More recently, photographic reproduction and digital images have facilitated our access to remote records. In many cases, the duplicate may be the only surviving copy. In other instances, it may be the only one to which we have access.

Beyond duplicates, *derivative works* take many forms that are, by nature, less reliable. The following spotlights critical differences as an original source is transformed into various derivatives.

- *Transcripts (transcriptions:* verbatim copies, manuscript or typed, attempt to render the words and punctuation just as the original scribe presented them. Documents found in the record books of town and county clerks are commonly transcripts made from original papers presented to the clerk for recording. Similarly, census marshals of the past often transcribed additional copies for submission to multiple offices. Such transcripts may be the best possible sources that remain today.

- *Edited transcripts:* more-or-less verbatim copies, usually pub-lished, typically apply editorial conventions that range from cor-rection of punctuation, grammar, and spelling to augmentation of facts. Published diaries, memoirs, and presidential papers are common examples that blur the traditional lines between "best" and "second-best" evidence. The "originals" themselves may or may not meet the other tests applied in this chapter's guidelines. Likewise the edited transcripts may be more or less trustworthy, depending upon the skill and integrity of the editor.

- *Abstracts:* abbreviated summaries of documents that ostensibly include all critical information, while eliminating only unnecessary verbiage.

- **Certified copies:** official copies with an added "certification," attesting that the document was officially prepared. The fact that a copy is "certified" does not necessarily mean that all details from the original are provided.

- **Certificates:** official copies created on a preprinted form whose blanks are populated with data from the original or the record copy. The preprinted format typically means that the source data is now rearranged to fit the form and that data from the source will be omitted if the certificate form has no blank for it.

- **Compendiums:** compilations of data gleaned from an assortment of related material, as often seen with published "vital records" from early American communities.

- **Databases and database entries:** digital finding aids that provide searchable access to pieces of data extracted from other sources or materials assembled from elsewhere.

- **Extracts:** portions of text quoted verbatim out of a record and enclosed in quotation marks. Unlike a transcript or abstract, extracts do not purport to represent all relevant information within the original. Extracts are selective, and they are precise. We quote, we don't paraphrase.

- **Nutshells:** very abbreviated abstracts that provide the gist of what a record is about, but do not include all relevant details.

- **Narrative accounts:** essays, genealogies, or histories supposedly based on facts taken from assorted records that authors have examined and reported through their own interpretative lenses. On the surface, their reliability is commonly judged by the degree to which compilers document each statement of fact with a reliable source.

- **Oral history:** family or legendary accounts passed down through the generations.

5

The reliability of a derivative work is influenced by the amount and type of processing it has undergone.

As careful researchers, we also consider the *processing* our information has gone through. A derivative work may be one or several steps removed from the original. A deed book in the town clerk's office could be the clerk's copy of the original documents or it could be a third-generation copy made when the first record book became timeworn. Cautious researchers always examine the inside covers, as well as initial and ending pages, of each record book for a possible clerical notation that the book has been recopied.

Each additional layer of processing adds the likelihood of transcription errors. The rank, post, title, or education of the individual who transformed the data can increase or reduce the likelihood of error, but it does not change the fact that each mutation is likely to be less accurate than the parent copy. Thus, we diligently track the ancestry of derivative works, hoping to trace each to its original source—at least to the earliest surviving version.

6

The purpose of a record and the motivation of its creators frequently affect its truthfulness.

Many documents are created for self-serving purposes, and all are produced by individuals of varing degrees of reliability. As careful researchers, we can take no record at face value. In appraising various types of materials, we apply such tests as these:

- *Affidavits or other sworn statements* (in a legal case, pension application, damage claim, etc.): To what extent did the complainants, defendants, or witnesses have cause for bias or gain?

- *Bible or diary entries:* Would the creator have had cause to misrepresent a fact? For example, a backdated marriage in the family Bible to hide a firstborn's "early" birth; or a diary entry that exaggerates the writer's role in the event because he or she anticipates that the diary will be made public.

7

The most reliable informants, as a rule, have first-hand knowledge of the events to which they testify.

Death certificates provide a classic example for illustrating this point. Let us say that the informant for a death certificate is the spouse of the deceased. We may logically expect the surviving spouse to have firsthand knowledge of the decedent's address, identity, and occupation. We would not expect the spouse to have firsthand knowledge of the decedent's birth, because it is improbable that the spouse was present at that birth. The spouse's knowledge of the person's birth date or place might be more accurately termed *hearsay*. On the other hand, the spouse's knowledge of the identity of the decedent's parents could be firsthand, if the spouse knew them personally.

8

The veracity and skill of a record's creator will have shaped its content.

Appraising this issue can be one of our most difficult tasks as a history researcher. It asks that we not only study the information inherent in a record but also acquaint ourselves with the scribe who penned the original document and any compiler(s) who prepared derivative works we have used. For example:

- *Local government records:* Does the court clerk's other work exhibit signs of care or carelessness? Might he be an unqualified or uninterested political appointee? As a case in point: Lew Wallace, the famed Civil War general and author of *Ben Hur,* was a lackadaisical fifteen-year-old school dropout—and son of the state governor—when he was appointed assistant clerk of Marion County, Indiana. His assignment: copying deeds and judgments at ten cents per hundred words.* Meticulously recorded documents from that place and time should not be expected.

9

Timeliness generally adds to a document's credibility.

Did months or years elapse between the event and the creation of the record that details it? As a rule of thumb (which may or may not hold true in any given case), a record created closer to the time of the event is less likely to contain errors than one created long after. Typical of the questions we apply in this regard are the following:

- *Affidavit for a U.S. military pension:* Was the application filed by, say, an amputee immediately after the end of his service, asking for a disability pension—or filed long after by a veteran claiming need in his old age? If filed by a widow, was she married to the veteran at the time he served, and thus knew of his service first-hand, or did she wed him in his dotage?

- *Family pages in a Bible:* What is the Bible's publication date? Is that date compatible with the first entry of family data, or has someone entered events from earlier years or generations? Are the ink and penmanship consistent throughout all the entries (an indication that they may have been made in one sitting), or are the entries recorded in hands of varying style and steadiness (an indication that they may have been recorded as they occurred, over the life span of one person or across several life spans)?

---

* Lew Wallace, *Lew Wallace: An Autobiography,* 2 vols. (New York: Harper & Brothers, 1906), vol. 1, chaps.7–8.

10

Penmanship should be studied for clues to identities, dates, and authenticity.

Being able to read the penmanship found in historic documents is still a basic skill for history researchers, but a sound *analysis* of penmanship goes far beyond a mere reading of the words. The manner in which letters are formed can be a distinctive characteristic of the person we are studying—or characteristic of a particular style of writing that person was taught. The types of pen nibs and ink, as well as the degree of pressure applied, can also help us determine when a document was created and whether portions of a document were all written by the same individual.

Records that seem relevant to a research problem should be evaluated from at least two standpoints.

Ancestral penmanship

For various reasons, individuals do authorize others to draft or sign documents in their names. Yet, as careful researchers, when we research a literate person or one who made a distinctive mark in lieu of an actual signature, we accumulate as many examples as possible of the manner in which they put pen to paper. Then we closely compare those instances. Significant variations between signatures or marks on documents that carry the same name must be logically explained, with supporting evidence, if we assert that all these documents were created by the same individual.

Scribal penmanship

Similarly, we appraise the handwriting used elsewhere within the record book or collection that contains the relevant document. A church register, for example, might appear to be an original, although it is actually an administrative copy—one in which additions or deletions might also have been made. So, we ask:

- Is the penmanship typical of the era in which the events occurred?

- Are all entries made in the same hand, or are there the variances one would expect from information entered over many months or years?

- Do original signatures appear on the recorded acts of marriage and baptism, as is common with many sacramental registers of past centuries?

- Are the entries recorded in a form-style book for a period in which such books were not the rule? Many preprinted registers, with blanks to be filled in, discreetly carry publication dates that may reveal their creation long after the original events occurred. These silently alert us to the fact that we are using derivative copies.

11

A record's custodial history affects its trustworthiness.

The annals of history are rife with cases of forged documents created long after the fact by someone with questionable intent. Affidavits, Bible records, deeds, letters, marriage bonds, and wills—these and more have been forged by people who had a need to "prove" the unprovable.

Protecting ourselves against deliberate fraud requires us to question each document we acquire: Is it in proper custody? Was it out of that custody at any time in its past? An imaged "document" that *should* be on public record but cannot be found in the appropriate record set is always suspect until proved valid by other means. The frequency with which fraudulent documents are discovered points to another reason why all manuscript materials need to be properly cited by name, book, page, file, collection, series, and repository.

As careful researchers, we also will consider the fact that even proper custody is no guarantee of authenticity or accuracy. Numerous instances exist of forged documents that have been filed legally, of spurious papers surreptitiously inserted into legal files long after the fact, and of baseborn alterations made to record books.

Modern technology has increased both the necessity and the difficulty of analyzing a document's authenticity. Artificial intelligence and even less sophisticated electronic tools permit the production of fake records of remarkable semblance to time-weathered materials. Enterprising firms and individuals are "recreating" ship rolls and other records for display, creations that appear to be original. Just as easily, the unscrupulous can add, to those redesigned rolls, passengers who never saw the ship. Couples can be posed together when, in real life, they were never joined by marriage, kinship, acquaintance, or even proximity. Imaging can obscure many characteristics that might, on the original document, give away fraud.

Reliable researchers are vigilant. They do not simply accept, assume, or trust without authentication.

12

All known records should be used and a thorough effort made to identify unknown materials.

A reliable analysis cannot be made from partial evidence. Any pertinent record or collection or repository that goes unconsulted is a silent bomb waiting to explode our premature theories. The risk is great enough when, in a run of luck, we are blessed with documents that all lean toward the same conclusion. The risk cannot be chanced when, as frequently happens, we have no direct evidence to support a conclusion but propose one through the assembly of indirect evidence.

13

The case is never closed on a historical or genealogical conclusion.

The reliable analysis of any piece of historical evidence is a complex process. As researchers, we repeat this process endlessly, applying the principles discussed in this chapter to every piece of evidence we find. We also recognize that no decision regarding identity, parentage, origin, or other "fact" can be considered definitive. Just as scientists revise their theories in the wake of new discoveries, so do historians. Any decision we make today could be changed tomorrow by the discovery of a new record.

In Sum:

There is no easy label—*trustworthy* or *suspect*—that researchers can apply to any document, much less any *type* of document. We cannot quantify the likelihood of reliability or assign probability scores to determine whether we should trust something we have found. A dubious factoid repeated a thousand times cannot outweigh an accurate fact from a single, impeccable source.

And so, we must mentally appraise the credibility of *each* assertion in *each* document on a detail-by-detail basis, considering all the factors outlined in this chapter. As we acquire historical and social perspective of each place and time, as we accumulate experience in evaluating the information we find, this phase of research becomes a less perplexing and more fascinating challenge.

*F*undamentals of Documentation

As we learned in Chapter 1: All sources are not created equal. Therefore, we need to forget the basic rule of source citation we learned when classroom teachers introduced us to the craft of writing research papers: We do not cite sources "so others will know where we got our information." We identify our sources—their strengths and their weaknesses—so *we* can reach the most reliable conclusions. *We document our work to help ourselves.* It's not a chore that hobgoblins of history require us to do for others.

This one point is so critical to our success that it deserves repeating:

> We do not cite sources "so others will know where we got our information." We identify our sources—their strengths and their weaknesses—so *we* can reach the most reliable conclusions. We document our work to help ourselves.

This chapter lays out thirteen guidelines upon which sound documentation is built.

Figure 2

uidelines for Documentation

1. Having *a* source to cite is not the objective; our goal is to find and cite the *best possible source.*

2. Any statement of fact that is not common knowledge must carry its own individual statement of source.

3. Source notes have two purposes: to identify the source of each piece of information; and to record details that affect the use or evaluation of both the source and its information.

4. Sources are tracked in two basic ways: by generic lists (bibliographies) and by source notes (aka reference notes) keyed to specific facts.

5. Source notes have two basic forms: full citations and shortened ones.

6. Source notes for narrative accounts can be presented in four ways: as footnotes, endnotes, hypertext, and parenthetical citations.

7. Source notes keyed to narrative text should be numbered consecutively and the corresponding numbers should appear in correct sequence within the text.

8. Explicit source notes should also be attached to family charts and data sheets.

9. Full citations should be placed on the front side of every imaged document and on every page of a research report.

10. We should not cite sources we have not used; it is both risky and unethical to "borrow notes" from other writers.

11. Even a full citation of source may not be sufficient, legally or ethically, when copying from another work.

12. Records imaged online require identification of both the original record and the online publisher of the images; details for each must be clearly separated.

13. Clear citations require attention to many details.

1

Having a source to cite is not the objective; our goal is
to find and cite *the best possible source.*

In the research stage, we want to record every source consulted,
regardless of our opinion of its value. Maintaining a track record
of all materials searched and all methods and strategies applied is
fundamental to all fields of research. Taking note of published or
widely circulated information that is clearly wrong is also wise; odds
are, we will need to refute it. But we are never justified in broadcast-
ing inaccurate or unproved information simply because we have a
source to cite for it.

Mere *citation* of a source proves nothing. When we recognize that a
source is deficient or that a better source should exist, the better
source should be sought and used. When we convert our raw notes
into an interpretative history or biography, we will want our information and our conclusions to be supported by sound evidence of
the highest quality possible.

2

Any statement of fact that is not common knowledge
must carry its own individual statement of source.

Distinguishing "common knowledge" from a fact that needs documentation is basically a matter of common sense. If we write that
the American Civil War erupted in 1861, that statement needs no
supporting evidence to attest its validity or to help locate the information. Most historical researchers know the year; and anyone else can
find it easily. However, a statement that John Smith enlisted on 23
August 1861 in Captain Hiram Jones's company of the Middletown

Mounted Volunteers would not be common knowledge. It requires a citation to a reliable source.

$$3$$

Source notes have two purposes:

- To identify the source of each piece of information by the four Ws of research: *Who? What? When? Where?*
- To record details that affect the use or evaluation of both the source and its information so we can answer the fifth W: *Why?*

Most researchers recognize the importance of the first purpose, although the formalities of citing those specifics may be confusing. Part Two of this manual addresses that problem.

The second purpose of citations—recording all details that affect the use or evaluation of the source and its information—is equally essential. Without those details we cannot answer the fifth basic *W* of research and reporting: *Why should we believe this source?*

As careful researchers, we need to expand many source citations to add observations not covered by the formal citation and to discuss related problems. The extent to which those explanations affect our judgment of a source, its information, or the evidence we draw from that information is a point made by the comparative notes in Figure 3.

In short: research is not a search for information or a simple recording of what we find. It is a search for truth, recognizing that truth is elusive. It is a search for reality, or as close to reality as we can get.

As we explore the past, at each step, we identify each document we image. We identify our source for each note we take and each statement we make in our reports, emails, letters, or blogs. If we do not, two results are certain: We will confuse ourselves, and we will mislead others.

Figure 3

*T*wo Functions
of a Source Note

Basic source citation to information from a journal article:

> 1. Mary Doe, "Vital Records: Freetown Deaths," *Ipswich Beginnings* 1 (Summer 1974): 12.

Expanded discussion to flag issues that affect reliability:

> 1. Mary Doe, "Vital Records: Freetown Deaths," *Ipswich Beginnings* 1 (Summer 1974): 12.

Doe's abstracts were not made from the actual vital records of Freetown. Rather, they were taken from "Research Notes of the Late Susie Smith," Smith Collection (MS, undated; at Anytown Public Library, Anytown, U.S.A.).

The folder containing this set of notes by Smith is labeled "Freetown Vital Records," but many of the given dates do not appear in the original vital-records register held by the Ipswich town clerk. The information that Mary Doe gives for John Smith on her page 12 is among the information *not* found in the original records book.

_____

Question: Which source note would help you the most?

4

Sources are tracked in two basic ways:
- Generic lists (bibliographies)
- Source notes (aka reference notes) keyed to specific facts

Bibliographies *are* generic master lists for quick consultation. They do not document any particular fact. Their primary purpose during research is to keep track of the materials we have examined. Their function in a published work is to provide the reader with a convenient list of the relevant resources used or suggested for further study.

Source notes (aka reference notes)—with complete and specific reference data—should be used when transcribing documents, making abstracts or research notes, imaging documents or photographs, preparing research reports (for our own files or for others), or composing historical narratives.

Part Two of this manual presents templates for citing a variety of materials in both bibliographic and source-note formats.

5

Source notes have two basic forms
- Full citations
- Shortened citations

In a narrative account, the first time we cite a source, we give full details. Our later citations to the same source will typically use a shortened form that is easily recognizable and quickly associated with both the full citation and the bibliographic entry.

When we transcribe, abstract, or image *records*, the use of shortened citations can be risky. If we take multiple excerpts from a single book, collection, or file, we should place a *full citation* on each sheet of our research notes and each image copy. With this precaution, if pages later become separated or shuffled, we (or others) will not be left wondering about the exact source of an assertion on any page.

For shortened citations to be beneficial, they must be simple—easy to grasp, easy to remember, and easy to find. Consequently, good researchers and writers avoid three common shortcuts that promote writer error and reader frustration:

Citing a source so briefly that it cannot be correctly identified

As an example, a "short citation" frequently seen in Louisiana-based articles, books, and research notes is **Mills, *Natchitoches*, 29** (or some other page number). However, five volumes with "Natchitoches" in the title have been published by three different Millses. A slight expansion to, say, *Natchitoches Colonials,* or *Natchitoches 1800–1826: Translated Abstracts* would take little more space and ensure that the reader can identify the source correctly.

This pitfall is particularly acute in history, where individuals often publish multiple volumes of abstracts from their local-area records. As a rule of thumb, a shortened citation for a local-records volume should not only cite the author but also extract from the title any words relating to *place, type of record,* and *time period.*

Reducing many source citations to acronyms or initialisms

This practice saves space, but it promotes confusion. Few readers can, or care to, retain a mental directory of KVR, QVRPX, LCTV, BWPC, LSNI, PMXE, and a dozen other mixtures of alphabet soup as they study a writer's work. Acronyms or initialisms are best restricted to those so widely used in the field that a key is hardly needed—as with national archives, national-level libraries, or national-level associations and their journals. Each short form should be fully identified the first time it appears, as demonstrated on page 23 with the initialism GPS. If numerous acronyms or initialisms are deemed necessary, a key should be added at the beginning of your manuscript or publication.

Referring readers to another note for its citation

When your note 72 needs to repeat something you previously said in your note 49, it can be tempting to simply say "see note 49." That shortcut will not be appreciated by readers. Source notes are distracting in the first place. Readers must break the train of thought they are following in the narrative, to search for a number amid the notes. When that sends them to yet another number simply because the writer did not want to retype the essential information, the annoyance tempts many readers to ignore the citations altogether.

Worse, the diligent reader who does follow the chain of citations to another note often finds that it does not match the text statement that launched the search. The cause is one danger inherent in this kind of citation: writers revise their drafts. They add, delete, and rearrange information—and they sometimes overlook adjusting statements in the corresponding notes. Modern word-processing applications revise reference numbers automatically to save writers a dreary chore. But when the text of a reference note reads "see note 49" and note 49 has been renumbered to 51, the internal mention of note 49 will not be automatically updated by the software.

6

Source notes for narrative accounts can be presented in four ways: as footnotes, endnotes, hypertext, and parenthetical citations.

The four options are not of equal merit:

- *Footnotes* are source citations that appear at the foot or bottom of each page. They are the standard for research reports and academic journals and are especially needed in books. Placing citations on the same page as the text they support encourages readers to compare assertions against the sources cited for them. It helps them appraise the soundness of the author's statements.

- **Endnotes** are source citations that appear at the end of an article or the end of a book. They are beloved by book publishers because they require less page space, thereby reducing costs. They are deplored by serious students of history who always consider each text statement against the cited source. Endnotes *are* appreciated by casual readers of history and biography who want an easy read, value "clean looking" pages, and are prone to accept whatever authors say without a critical appraisal. They are also simply ignored by most readers who have no patience with flipping back and forth to the end of a work to find the appropriate endnotes. If you choose endnotes, a word of caution: Do not put any discussions there that you actually want your reader to read.

- **Hypertext** is used today within many electronic publications as a form of endnotes with some benefits of footnotes. At each reference number, an embedded link enables readers to click once and immediately see the corresponding note (or chart, graph, appendix, etc.) in full. However, when digital files containing hypertext are printed, the hypertext links are lost; thus, the documentation is lost. Until software producers remedy this problem, hyperlinks will not be the usual choice for serious research.

- **Parenthetical citations** are short-form citations embedded in the narrative, as with **(Smith, 23)** to indicate that a quotation or piece of information came from page 23 of a publication by an author named Smith who is cited on an attached bibliography. This type of citation is common in scientific papers where all citations are to simply cited published works (and a relatively small number of those). They are unworkable for history researchers and writers who use hundreds or thousands of sources for a project, with heavy emphasis on original documents that are complicated to cite.

7

Source notes keyed to narrative text should be numbered consecutively and the corresponding numbers should appear in correct sequence within the text.

Source numbering within text is simple. Most word-processing software does it automatically, creating superscript reference numbers in our text wherever we need them. Those numbers are always sequential. Multiple reference numbers never appear in the same spot, and each number is matched to its own footnote or endnote.

Traditionally in expository writing, note numbers within the text have been placed at the *end of sentences*, outside the closing punctuation marks. Indeed, most publishers prefer a single note at the *end of a paragraph* to cover all issues within that paragraph. That convenience for the publisher, however, is antithetical to sound historical research and reporting. For clarity and exactness, Evidence Style citations follow these two practices:

- *When a sentence contains information from more than one source,* each with information the other does not offer, each reference number is placed at the point where information from that source actually ends. (See figure 4, reference numbers 2 and 3.) If all of a sentence is supported by multiple sources, then a single citation at the end of the sentence would be appropriate.

- *When a sentence contains not only information from a specific source but also our personal interpretation or observations,* we place the reference note at the point where the source's information ends and our amplification begins.

In both cases, the source number should appear immediately after the punctuation mark that divides the two parts of the sentence. When creating a narrative genealogy, *a superscript source number*

Figure 4

Placement of Note Numbers

Text and corresponding footnotes:

John[1] Jones, the developer of Boulder's best-known saloon, was born about 1837 in Glasgow, Scotland.[1] Allegedly, he migrated to the U.S. the year that civil hostilities ended[2] and settled first in Midville, Missouri, where he operated a shoe shop at the time of the 1870 census.[3] With a wife Mary, who remains unidentified, he ....

---

1. Any County (Whatever State), Naturalization Book 3: 25, declaration of intention filed 27 July 1873 by John Jones; County Clerk's Office, Countyseat.

2. Mary (Smith) Jones Diary, owned 2025 by her great-great-granddaughter Merry Schmit James (111 First Street, Midville, MO 00000).

3. 1870 U.S. census, Any County, Missouri, population schedule, village of Midville, page 2, dwelling 11, family 17; imaged online, *Family Search* (https://www.familysearch.org/search/collection/1438024 : accessed 1 January 2025).

In the text above, the superscript number following the name *John* denotes generation number. It appears in italics to distingish it from reference note numbers that conventionally are set in roman type. Some numbering systems use other conventions to make this distinction between generation numbers and reference note numbers.

should never appear directly after a given name, unless there is intervening punctuation, because the superscript position immediately after a given name is the place genealogy reserves for an individual's generation number. (See John[1] in figure 4.)

8

Explicit source notes should also be attached to family charts and data sheets.

This chapter's Guideline 2 (any statement of fact that is not common knowledge must carry its own individual statement of source) is blithely ignored by many writers, publishers, and typesetters when they create family charts and data sheets. However, nothing about these mechanical formats overwrites our (or our readers') need for that source information.

As a compromise, some publishers append to a chart (or data sheet) a generic list of, say, thirty-nine sources from which that chart or sheet's ninety-two names, dates, and places have been extracted. This halfway measure does not meet standards or the needs of those who use our work. No assertion on that sheet can be evaluated—its reliability cannot be appraised—unless its source is identified. Forcing oneself or others to comb a list of dozens of references to identify the source of one item of information is a thoughtless disregard of everyone's time.

Guideline 8 goes one step beyond Guideline 2. When conflicting information from equally credible sources exists for a single date, event, or relationship and the discrepancy has not been resolved, the chart or the data sheet should record and separately document each piece of information. Arbitrarily choosing one fact over another in order to fit something into the limited space on a form, while relegating conflicting data to notes in another location, is a common cause of research problems.

Both genealogists and historians who reconstruct communities, when they choose computer software to compile their data sheets and charts, should choose carefully with an eye toward documentation capability for all forms or reports the software generates.

9

Full citations should be placed on the front side of every imaged document and on every page of a research report.

Researchers who overlook this caution cause themselves and others much unnecessary grief. No one wishes to mar or alter the face of a document. Nor should they. In that spirit, many careful researchers place their documentation on the reverse side. As that imaged copy goes into circulation, the inevitable happens: someone in the circulation chain fails to copy the back side of the record. Thereafter, no one who receives it will know its source. Penning or typing the documentation into the *margin* of the image's face will prevent this problem. If adequate margin does not exist, modern editing software allows for the enlargement of margins.

Similar problems occur when researchers create research notes in word-processing software. With research notes and research reports, we do a disservice to our readers (and ourselves in the future) if we identify the research repository only on the report's first page, or fully identify a source only the first time it is used. Once the notes are reduced to hard copy and circulated, those sheets will inevitably become shuffled and individual pages will stray into other places. At that point the complete source information is lost. If the report is circulated in electronic form, the cut-and-paste adaptations made by users will separate one research note from another, and the notes that lack full documentation will then become mystery objects that frustrate everyone.

10

We should not cite sources we have not used; it is both
risky and unethical to "borrow notes" from other writers.

As researchers, we have all heard that original sources are the "gold standard." However, we cite that "gold standard" only if we use it. When we use a published source or other derivative works and the author provides a citation to an original document, it is neither safe nor ethical for us to cite what the other author used unless we actually consult it. We must cite what *we* use, and credit should always be given where it is due. By the same token, we would not wish to inherit the blame for an error another writer made when using a record *we* have not seen.

An acceptable practice for us would ordinarily be one or both of the following:

- Record the details as they appear in the earlier writer's work; identify that work fully; then note that the writer cites his or her source as [*whatever*]. In this portion of our citation, we copy the earlier writer's citation exactly, placing it within quotation marks.

- Consult the cited material to verify that the writer has reported the information correctly and to determine whether there is additional information to be gleaned.

If the derivative source we first used cites an original record, we should indeed follow the second option: examine the original and cite it as our own reference. If the derivative source gave us special insight into the use or interpretation of the original, we should also credit the earlier writer for this insight. If the original material is of a nature that we might not have found it on our own, we may wish to credit the prior writer for calling this material to our attention. If on the other hand, the earlier work erroneously reports the facts from the original, then that error should be explained and corrected in a discussion added to our source note.

11

**Even a full citation of source may not be sufficient,
legally or ethically, when copying from another work.**

Crediting other authors, or properly citing the whereabouts of specific documents, may not be adquate protection for us if we publish or otherwise circulate our research. The issues of copyright, plagiarism, and fair use also come into play. There are strict but fuzzy limits to the amount of material we can quote from another source. Some publishers require permission—as well as acknowledgment in our citation—if more than a specified number of words are copied. Some set other restrictions. The following rules of thumb are reasonably safe guidelines:

- When copying more than *three words* from another source, we treat those words as a quote. Stylistically, if the quote is short—three lines or less—we weave the quote into our text, setting it off with quotation marks. If the material is longer than three lines, we set it off in an indented paragraph. In either case, the source of the quote should be clearly identified. The use of another person's words, thoughts, or material without giving them credit is *plagiarism.*

- When using more than *three paragraphs* from another source, we obtain permission from the author and the publisher. If permission is granted, our credit line acknowledges that permission. If permission is not granted then, of course, we do not use the quote.

- When quoting from *manuscript material* owned by an individual, agency, or institution, we also seek permission. Some archives severely limit copying, quoting, or publishing from their collections.

Stripped Bare Guide

In applying these guidelines, we should also consider two other questions that relate to the Fair Use Doctrine:*

- What is the proportion of our copied material in comparison to the body of information from which we have taken this material? Court decisions rarely uphold reuse of more than a small fraction of the whole.

- What effect will our circulation of this material have upon the market for the original? Even if our own work is distributed without charge, its availability will affect the market for the original.

The issue here is not whether *we* make money off the other person's work. The issue is whether our publication of that work will affect the other person's return on their own labor and the other person's right to determine how their own work is presented.

12

Records imaged online require identification of both the original record and the online publisher of the images; details for each must be clearly separated.

Source citation has been greatly complicated by the emergence of digital imaging and electronic media as modes of publication. When we examine record images online and attempt to define the elements our citations should include, we keep in mind that this material commonly has two parts we must identify:

- Most such material *originated in manuscript or book form*. It may have been created in modern times or it may be older writings.

- Most such material is now being *published* by a firm or agency that was not the original creator.

---

* 17 U.S. Code § 107 – "Limitations on exclusive rights: Fair Use"; HTML edition, Cornell Law School, *LII Legal Information Institute* (https://www.law.cornell.edu/uscode/text/17/107 : accessed 1 January 2025).

Therefore, a citation to material reproduced online will have at least two parts (i.e., two layers):

- a citation to the original; and
- a citation to the online publication.

The sequence of the two layers are interchangeable, but the details within each layer are not.

Part Two of this guide covers layers and citation formats in specific detail. The important issues to remember at this point are these:

- When websites offer historical material, we always clearly distinguish between *imaged records* and a publisher's *database details*.

- Details that identify the publisher and its database are not mixed into the layer in which we identify the original. The two are separate entities, with separate creators, and the distinction between them must be preserved.

13

Clear citations require attention to many details.

Mies van der Rohe once declared, "God is in the details!" He spoke of the building blocks of architecture, not those of a source citation; but his observation still applies. Beyond the main points covered in this chapter, a variety of other details ensure a clear recording and reporting of our references.

Correct bibliographic data

The title page should be consulted to identify a book's name properly. Spines and covers often carry shortened titles. If the work is no longer at hand when we realize that we need additional publication data, we can seek fuller details from the Library of Congress's online catalog of copyrighted publications at loc.gov or the more comprehensive

Worldcat.org. If we do so, we must be careful to ensure that we have identified the exact edition that we used.

Latin "shorthand"

Latin terms are rarely used today as a means of shortening reference citations. *Op. cit., supra, infra,* and *cf.* are now obsolete idioms few researchers can even define. Two other Latinisms are holdovers: *sic* (which means "There's an error here that I'm copying exactly but I'm pointing it out so you won't think the error is mine") and *ibid.* (an abbreviation for *ibidem*). Several particulars need to be borne in mind when using the latter:

- *Ibid.* means "in the same source as above."

- *Ibid.* is not used if the prior note cites multiple references.

- *Ibid.* is not used if the prior note has a discussion as well as a citation to a source.

- *Ibid.* is not used until your final manuscript is prepared. If used in preliminary drafts, a rearrangement of your notes or an insertion or deletion of a sourced statement in the text can separate an *ibid.* from the preceding note to which it refers. Thereafter, the citation represented by that *ibid.* would be incorrect.

Capitalization

Capitalization of titles varies according to circumstances and to international customs. It is useful to remember the following:

- **Font style:** Setting a title entirely in capital letters is frowned upon—an offense to typography because it crowds the lines of type and visually overwhelms the reader's eyes. For similar reasons, the underlining of titles has also been discouraged. In modern typography, italics are standard for the titles of books, journals, websites, CDs, and other standalone publications. (See Stylistic Tips for Source Notes, Figure 6).

- **Font-style substitutions:** When typing online in forums that are still ASCII based, limitations may require an exception to the above rule. Capitalization may be substituted for italics in a book title whenever italics cannot be generated by the platform in use. If the book title is long, consisting of both a main title and a subtitle, you may capitalize only the main title and then, after the colon that separates the two parts of the title, render the subtitle in ordinary mixed-case roman type.

- **Language differences:** English-language titles use initial capitals for all words except (*a*) articles that appear as the first word of the title or subtitle, (*b*) coordinating conjunctions such as *and* or *but*, and (*c*) prepositions. French titles capitalize only the first word. (American library catalogers generally follow this practice also, although it has not been accepted by most American style manuals for writing and publishing.) German-language titles capitalize only the first word and nouns. When working in languages other than your own, it is always a good idea to analyze the patterns used in major publications within that language.

- **Published gremlins:** When the title page of a book uses incorrect capitalization, it is permissible to correct the usage in our citations. We cannot change the *words* of the title, but we can appropriately capitalize them.

- **Punctuation:** If the title of a book or article ignores punctuation conventions or omits diacritical marks, it is permissible to correct the problem. If we do not, our own readers will assume *we* have committed the offense.

- **Unpublished material vs. publications:** Many rules of citation require us to distinguish between published and unpublished materials. The lines continue to blur as new media develop. As a rule of thumb at present:

  > *Published* material is material disseminated in print, put into microform for circulation, reduced to electronic disks, or placed

online for access by others. Material published online may be open on the web or behind a paywall.

> *Unpublished material* may exist in the same forms but may have been produced only for preservation or for very limited sharing.

To illustrate: a set of estate papers in the recorder's office of a county courthouse might exist in these varied forms:

Original loose papers .... unpublished

Original manuscript volumes .... unpublished

Electronic images accessed via a
    courthouse computer station .... unpublished

Microfilmed copies of loose papers or packets,
    accessed at the courthouse.. unpublished

Microfilmed copies supplied to a state archive
    without permission to rent or sell copies..................... unpublished

Microfilmed copies supplied to *FamilySearch*
    without permission to rent, sell, or place online .... unpublished

Imaged copies created by *FamilySearch*
    without permission to place on the open web .... unpublished

Imaged copies placed freely online by *FamilySearch*
    with the consent of the owner of the record set .... published

Figure 5

Abbreviation Tips

Standard abbreviations:

assn.	= *association*	n.p.	=	*No Publisher*
bpt.	= *baptized*			*No Publication Place*
bk.	= *book*	NS	=	*New series, New style*
chap.	= *chapter*	OS	=	*Old Series, Old Style*
Co.	= *County, Company*	pt.	=	*part*
col.	= *column*	p./pp.	=	*page(s)*
comp.	= *compiler*	p.p.	=	*privately printed*
c./ca.	= *circa*	reg.	=	*register*
dept.	= *department*	rev. ed.	=	*revised edition*
ed.	= *edition, editor*	RG	=	*record group*
eds.	= *editors*	sect.	=	*section*
et al.	= *and others*	ser.	=	*series*
fo.	= *folio*	supp.	=	*supplement*
ff.	= *and following*	transcr.	=	*transcriber*
MS/MSS	= *manuscript(s)*	transl.	=	*translator*
no.	= *number*	v./vs.	=	*versus*
n./nn.	= *note(s)*	ver.	=	*version*
n.d.	= *no publication date*	vol.	=	*volume*

Other considerations

1. State names may be abbreviated traditionally or with two-letter postal codes.
2. Page numbers need not be preceded by *p.* when citing books and articles. When citing censuses, newspapers, or other materials that involve references to several types of numbers (*e.g.*, p. 37, line 24; *or* p. 3, col. 2), the inclusion of *p.* before the page number will help clarify the situation.
3. Professional credentials (postnominals) following personal names are usually written as initialisms with no periods. Academic credentials have traditionally carried periods, but that tradition is frequently ignored today.
4. Abbreviations should be avoided within narrative text, except for titles of address such as Mr., Mrs., or Rev.
5. Abbreviations do not save a significant amount of space. The thoughtful writer avoids all but the truly obvious.

Stripped Bare Guide

Figure 6

tylistic Tips
for Source Notes

1. *Italics,* used in the name of a source, signifiy that it is a
   - standalone publication (book, CD-ROM, fiche, film, journal, map, etc.); or
   - published court case

2. *Quotation marks,* used around the name of a source, signify
   - a manuscript, dissertation, or thesis that is unpublished;
   - an article within a periodical (journal, magazine, newspaper, etc.); or
   - a chapter within a book

   Although newspapers have traditionally put quotation marks around book titles, that practice is not generally followed elsewhere.

3. *Ellipses* (three dots, with spaces before, between, and after) signify that part of the original title or quoted passage is deleted.

4. *Square brackets* [ ] signify that the editor or transcriber has added words not in the original source. Parentheses should never be substituted.

5. *Angle brackets* < > are no longer used in historical writing because they conflict with technological uses.

6. *Capitalization* should be limited to proper nouns. It is not necessary to capitalize *volume, book, roll, census,* or other words describing part of a source unless those parts fall within a formal title that is placed in quotation marks or italics.

7. *Postnominals* (initials appearing after personal names to indicate professional credentials and academic degrees) are written in capitals that are reduced in size to the height of the *x* in the font being used. Credentials outside the field are not normally cited unless they relate to the subject on which the author writes (e.g., an M.D. who writes on genetics).

Figure 7

Bibliographic Tips

When compiling a list of sources:

1. Apply the guidelines found under Stylistic Tips, Figure 6.

2. Subdivide the list into at least two categories: "Original Sources" and "Derivative Works." You may further divide this source list as needed to organize your sources.

3. List works in alphabetical order, by author, within each section. If no author is known for a particular work, the title becomes the first cited element and its first word determines its alphabetical placement. If a title begins with *A, An,* or *The,* alphabetization is by the first letter of the second word.

4. Group together all works by the same author.

5. For authors of multiple works, don't repeat the author's name in each listing. You should cite the author fully in the first instance only. Subsequent listings use three 3-em dashes (i.e., a dash whose length corresponds to three times the width of your font's *m*) in place of the author's name. If em dashes are not available in your software, an underscore of that same length may be substituted. See Appendix 2 for examples.

6. If an author produced some works alone and some with other writers, first group all those produced alone, and then group all those published under joint authorship, listing them thereunder alphabetically by the surname of the second author. Again, three 3-em dashes are used for the already cited primary author instead of repeating the name.

7. Do not number items on a bibliography. You may do so on a source list for use in a classroom, lecture hall, or webinar setting in which audiences are referred to the sources amid the presentation.

*P*art Two:
Constructing Citations

*C*onstruction Basics

Citations to historical sources can be simple, as when citing a basic book or an article from a newspaper or journal. They can also be complicated. In fact (but don't let this point scare you), *most* sources cited by history researchers *are* complicated because of two things:

- *History researchers use many original documents that are not published.* Identifying them calls for considerable detail in order to distinguish each document from hundreds or millions of others in the same archive.

- *Many of these original documents are now being imaged online.* While desktop access to distant archives is a fantastic boon to our research, it complicates our citations. Each time we cite an online document, we have *two* entities to identify—the original document and the website that provides the document—each with its own identity and organizational scheme.

Most complicated matters—even citations—can be stripped down to their bare essentials. That is the purpose of this chapter. In simple language, it will walk you through

1. the three citation types used by history researchers;

2. the five questions every citation must answer: *Who, What, When, Where,* and *Why should we believe this information?;*

3. the seven building blocks of a citation that you can mix and match as needed;

4. the concept of *layered* citations, which have always existed for archived records and are now essential when citing online documents;

5. how to use the building blocks and layers to identify any type of source in any corner of the world.

1

Three citation types cover all needs for history researchers.

Every citation need we have as history researchers can be handled using one of these three types:

- ***First (Full) Reference Notes:*** These are used for both footnotes and endnotes. Specifically, we use a full citation the first time we cite a source within a piece of writing. We also use this format for the citations we put on documents (i.e., the document labels).

- ***Subsequent (Shortened) Reference Notes:*** After we have cited a source in full, we may use a shorter version of that citation each time we need to cite it again.

- ***Source List Entries:*** We use these on our master list of materials consulted but rarely use them elsewhere.

The First Reference Note is the default for history researchers.

For notetaking, document labeling, and writing, the First Reference Note is where we record all details that identify the evidence for each assertion we make.

2

Every citation must answer the 5 *W*s.

Every citation needs to tell its reader five things—the classic five *W*s followed by every good reporter: *Who? What? When? Where?* and *Why?* For researchers, the *Why* question is quite specific and immensely important: *Why should we and others believe this bit of information I'm taking from this source?*

Each piece of information in a citation is there to answer one of these five questions. A single citation may address some questions multiple times. For example:

- **The Who? question** prompts us to identify (*a*) the entity that created the source; (*b*) the entity that edited the source; and (*c*) the entity that published the source.

- **The What? question** prompts us to identify not only the *title* of the source but also the *nature* of what we are citing.

- **The When? question** prompts us to identify (*a*) the date a document was created; or (*b*) the date a publication was published.

- **The Where? question** prompts us to identify (*a*) where a book or website is *published*; or (*b*) where a unique record is *held*; and (*c*) *where within* the source we found the specific piece of information—that is, the page, figure, entry number, image number, etc.

The details we record for each of the first four *W*s also help us answer the extremely important fifth *W*: *Why should we believe this piece of information?*

- **The Who?** details of a citation speak to the veracity or experience

63

of the creator. These details are often our first measure of whether information might be reliable.

- **The What?** details that we record in a citation include more than just the name by which a record is called. If a formal title exists, that title speaks to the nature of the information we take from that source. For example, if the title identifies our source as tax records of the city of Milwaukee, then our citation needs to convey whether the source presents actual images of the original tax rolls or someone's abstracts that might contain serious misreadings, omissions, or even additions. If the title is too generic, we may also need to add a descriptor to that title to record other relevant details.

- **The When?** details we report for a book or manuscript can be critical to our evaluation of its content. For example, a book titled *Early Times in Queensland, 1820–1860*, published in 1861, might offer memoirs of a person who lived there through those years. That same title could also be used for a 2024 history of Queensland, as interpreted by a remote writer mining random online records. Or an 1861 memoir of that name could have been reissued in 2020 with editorial additions and deletions. The relationship between content and its author, as explained by our *When?* details, can be critical to our *Why should I believe this?* answer.

- **The final Why?** question applies to every "fact" or opinion we copy or assert. If the situation warrants, our answer to *Why should this be believed?* may be detailed in a separate sentence or para- graph following the citation, as shown in last chapter's Figure 3.

3

With seven building blocks, you can construct any kind of citation.

These seven building blocks create the structure of all citations, regardless of the type of source we are citing. Each building block answers one of the critical *W* questions:

1. Creator (*Who?*)
2. Title (*What?*)
3. Descriptor (*What?*)
4. Place (*Where?*)
5. Publisher (*Who?*)
6. Date/Year (*When?*)
7. Specific Item (*Where within?*)

Each building block has its own field in a citation and sometimes more than one field. However, every citation does not use every building block. For example, citations to original manuscripts do not identify publishers because manuscripts, by definition, are unpublished.

How these building blocks are assembled depends primarily upon whether we are citing

- published works;
- unpublished manuscripts and artifacts; or
- imaged media made from the above.

Punctuation and formatting will also vary according to those three broad groups, a point that will be demonstrated in the next chapter as each template is presented.

Block 1: Creator (*Who?*)

All sources have a creator. That creator may be a person or a corporate, governmental, or social agency. The creator may fill one of various roles such as *author, compiler, editor, translator,* etc. There may be multiple creators filling the same role or multiple creators filling different roles. By convention, authorship is the default. Authors are cited without an explicit role stated for them; all other creators should be identified according to their role.

If the identity of the author is unknown, we may use the word *Anonymous* in the Creator Block or simply leave this block blank.

Websites may be *eponymous* (self-named), in which case it would be redundant to cite the name in both the Creator Block and the Title Block (and likely in the URL/Place Block, as well). Omitting the Creator Block for self-named sites reduces repetition and length.

Block 2: Title (*What?*)

After our citation identifies the creator of the source, we will then identify *what* that person or agency created. This will be either the title shown on the source (which we quote exactly) or, if the source is untitled, an identifier we create using our own words.

Three practices govern the way in which we format words in the Title Block. These typographic conventions matter, because each conveys a distinctive message.

- *Italics* identify titles of *standalone publications* such as books, CDs or DVDs, maps that are individually published, musical compositions, periodicals (journals, magazines, newspapers), plays, and websites.

- *Quotation marks* identify titles for *parts* of a standalone publication—e.g., the title of a chapter in a book, an article in a periodical, or a database or article at a website.

- *Initial capitalization* of the first word, with no italics or quote marks, is used when we create an identifier for an untitled manuscript.

Block 3: Descriptor (*What?*)

Many titles need an additional descriptor that is not part of its formal title. This descriptor more clearly identifies the source or helps with source analysis. Common situations include these:

- *Editions:* When we cite a book that has been issued in multiple editions, the Descriptor Block identifies the edition used.

- *Journal articles:* When we cite an article within a journal, we use a Descriptor Block immediately after the title to identify the exact volume number in which the article appears.

- **Multivolume works:** When we cite a book that has multiple volumes, we use a Descriptor Block after the title to state the number of volumes in that set. If, say, we have access to only one of those volumes, then our Descriptor Block would identify the specific volume we used.

- **Series:** When we cite a book that is part of a series, the series is named in the Descriptor Block. Neither quotation marks nor italics are used for a series name. Headline-style capitalization (capitalizing all words except articles and prepositions) is used to convey the fact that the series title is a formal title created by the author or publisher.

- **Website items:** When we cite an item at a website, if its title does not clearly identify its nature, we use the Descriptor Block to specify whether it is an article, a database (with or without images), a map, a user-contributed family tree at a commercial website, etc.

The title's Descriptor Block is always placed immediately after the title it describes. A comma typically separates the two blocks.

Block 4: Place of Creation, Publication, or Access (*Where?*)

Every source is rooted somewhere. That information is often critical to the identification of the creator or the publisher. This *Where* usually can be gleaned from the source itself. For example:

CREATION PLACE:
- **Diaries and personal journals** frequently include details that identify the author's locale.
- **Letters** typically include the date on which they were written and the place where the writer was at that time.

PUBLICATION PLACE:
- **Published books and periodicals,** on their title page or in a copyright notice placed on the reverse of the title page, cite the city and state or province where the publisher is located.

- *Web pages and websites* are distinctly identified by a web address that identifies exactly where they can be found online. However, the architecture of many websites requires us to wade through a minefield of choices. For detailed guidance, see below for "Online Publications: Special Issues for Answering *Where.*"

ACCESS PLACE:

Whether we cite an access place depends upon the type of source we are using. As a general rule:

- *Artifacts, documents, manuscripts, and other one-of-a-kind items* must always be cited to a location where they can be accessed.

- *Publications* are rarely cited to a physical place of access because the act of publication has made them available in many locales.

- *Published images, used online,* are not cited to their physical location as though we personally used them in their archival setting. If the online provider of those images identifies the physical location of the original records, then our final layer of the citation reports what the provider states, and we clearly convey the fact that we are reporting secondhand information.

ONLINE PUBLICATIONS: SPECIAL ISSUES FOR ANSWERING *WHERE?*

Identification of a website's address—its Uniform Resource Locator (URL)—can be tricky. Long URLs often represent dynamic pages created on the fly when we enter a search term. A long URL may work for us only so long as we do not clear our computer's browser cache—in which case it will not work for others.

- **Capitalization:** Many URLs are case sensitive. We should copy a URL exactly, with no corrections of capitalization or alteration of style. When a URL appears at the beginning of a sentence, as in bibliographic entries, we should not capitalize the first letter.

- **Dashes, hyphens, tildes and underlines:** We should take special care in reproducing em dashes (—), en dashes (–), hyphens (-), tildes (~), and underlines (__). Each has a distinct coding, and one cannot be substituted for the other in a URL.

- **Line breaks and punctuation:** When it is necessary to break a URL at the end of the line, we should use our software's soft-break process. We should never hyphenate a line break in the URL or allow our software to do so automatically.

  If a URL contains a hyphen, we break the line immediately *before* the hyphen, not after. Leaving a hyphen at the end of a line, within the URL, triggers questions as to whether the hyphen was intended. A soft-break may be made between syllables or after a colon, slash, or double slash. However, if we need to soft-break the line near any other embedded punctuation mark, then the break we create should place the punctuation mark at the start of the next line.

  In Evidence Style citations, URLs are followed by *space-colon-space,* and then the appropriate date of publication, revision, or access. This practice follows the practice already used in library cataloging, whereby a book's publication place is followed by a space, then a colon, then a space before the date. The space between the URL and the colon creates a clear and finite break between the URL and other punctuation that might follow it under present or future protocols.

- **PALS and ARKs:** Major providers of online document images are experimenting with "persistent identifiers"—variously dubbed PALs and ARKs—with a hope toward creating permanent links. The resulting URLs are relatively short in most cases. While permanancy has not yet been achieved, PALs and ARKs provide reasonably durable links to specific pages or images and, thus, are much more helpful to users than links that point only to a root page.

- **Paths and waypoints:** An alternative to long URLs is to cite the website's home page (or the database's launch page) plus the *path* that takes us to the item of interest. That path will consist of *waypoints*: specific words used in the website's menus through which we navigate to arrive at the specific item we need. We should always copy the wording, capitalization, and punctuation of waypoints exactly.

Our recitation of a path and its waypoints is placed immediately after our parenthetical statement of the URL and date, and each waypoint is introduced by a greater-than sign. For example:

> 1. "Oklahoma County Marriages, 1890–1995," database with images, *FamilySearch* (https://familysearch.org/ark: /61903/3:1:9Q97-Y3Q7-Z6Y : accessed 1 January 2025) > **digital film 4532716 > image 479 of 711.**

Block 5: Publisher (*Who?*)

Place and *date* have traditionally represented the essentials for citing published works. However, the more generic term *publication data* also calls for the name of the publisher. As best practices:

- **Book, CD-DVD, and map citations** should identify publishers. The practice of omitting publisher names (a practice often seen within academic publications) began on the premise that scholars will cite well-known, authoritative works from major publishing houses or other academic presses that are easily located from just the identification of the publisher's city. Both assumptions are no longer valid. In fact, in this digital age, publishers do not always identify their physical location; their name rather than their location has become the most essential information.

- **Journal and magazine citations** rarely cite publishers. When we feel that a journal or magazine might not be adequately identified from its too-generic title, we add further identification in the Descriptor Block following the title.

- **Newspaper citations** do not identify publishers. The publisher's name and newspaper's name are usually one and the same.

- **Website and blog citations** typically do not include publishers because the publisher is usually the creator.

Block 6: Date or Year of Creation or Publication (*When?*)

Placing each source in the context of *time* is critical not only to its identity but also to our analysis of that source. Sources may carry multiple dates, representing multiple actions at different times. For example:

- **Original records** (both personal and public) usually carry a date on which the document was written, begun, or completed. *This date is an essential part of the document's identification.*

- **Original registers (record books)** maintained by churches or government agencies frequently carry labels on the cover or spine stating when the clerk began the register and perhaps the day or year the last entry was made. When a register's cover carries no identification, or the cover has been torn away, we might find a label or title on the first inside page. With undated church and governmental registers, we may glean the span of years from the recording dates of the first and last documents. *This date or time frame is an essential part of the record book's identification.*

- **Individual documents or entries within registers** will carry their own dates and sometimes multiple dates. A deed, will, or other recorded legal document may state (*a*) the date the document was created, (*b*) the date it was presented to the court for proving and recording, and (*c*) the date it was actually recorded. *All these dates are important to the analysis process and should be included in the research notes made for that record.*

Similarly, *publication* dates are essential to the correct identification of a published work. They can also be critical to analyzing the validity of statements therein. The fullness of the date we cite will vary according to the type of publication. Generally speaking:

- **Books** are cited by the year of the publication, which is typically stated on the book's title page or copyright page. When books are reprinted or revised long after their original date of publication, we include both publication dates.
- **Journals and magazines** typically carry a month or season, as well as a year. Both should be cited.
- **Newspapers** typically carry an exact day, month, and year. That full date should be cited.
- **Web pages, websites, and online blogs** may (or may not) carry dates of creation, publication, or revision. If one is stated, we cite that date and say what the date represents. If we cannot discern a date, then we cite our date of access. Web-based materials are edited frequently and often silently. The access date identifies which version we used. Therefore, it is useful to record both the publication or revision date *and* the access date—with the latter indicating that the information we are citing still existed online "as late as" that access date.

Block 7: Specific Item (*Where Within?*)

Reference note citations, because they are keyed to specific assertions in our text, should state exactly *where within* a source the supporting evidence can be found. As general guidelines:

- **Book citations** usually cite page or figure numbers. A volume number may or may not be appropriate. For example:
  > If the book is a multivolume work and our Descriptor Block cites the total number of volumes, then our Specific Item Block will identify the *specific volume* and page number, with a colon separating the two—e.g., 7:231 or 7: 231. (Whether to place a space after the colon that separates the two numbers is a style choice.)
  > If the Descriptor Block for a multivolume work cites one specific volume, then our Specific Item Block does not have to repeat the volume number. Only the page number is needed.

- *Journal article citations* typically cite page or figure numbers. They may also cite the page range for the full article before calling attention to one specific item or page.
- *Newspaper citations* typically cite page and column numbers. For modern newspapers that have multiple sections (e.g., "Lifestyle" and "Finance" or "Section A" and "Section B"), the section identifier should be stated immediately before the page and column numbers—e.g.: Lifestyle section, page 3, column 4.
- *Original-document citations* handle pagination in different ways. For example:
  > If we are generically discussing the full manuscript, then a specific page number might not be appropriate.
  > If the manuscript consists of only a small page or two of legible script, a specific page citation might be unnecessary.
  > When the document consists of more than two pages, best practice calls for citing the specific page from which we took that specific information.
  > When working with original files or packets containing multiple documents, our reference note should cite fully the specific document from which we extracted the specific piece of information we are using.
- *Web pages, blogs, and other unpaginated online materials* may be cited to a specific paragraph or to a section head.

4

Layered citations create separation and flexibility.

The concept of layered citations has always existed, although it has not been labeled as such. Traditionally,

- layers have been used for citing manuscripts with complex archival descriptions that require identification of the document, the file, the collection, the series, the record group, etc. Each of these represent a layer.

- layers have also been used in citations to published works that string several sources into the same sentence.

For clarity in both situations, convention dictates that the details describing one layer be separated from the next layer with a semicolon.

Single-layer Citations

In Evidence Style, citations to print-published materials and simple web publications use the same format. Both can be handled in a single layer. For example:

- *Books, journal and magazine articles, maps, newspaper items, and other standalone publications,* when we consult the physical form, need only a single layer. (See Templates 1–5, next chapter.)

- *Blogs and websites that create their own material,* such as articles and simple databases, require only one layer. (Template 1)

  However, website offerings must be carefully analyzed to determine the nature of what we are using. Many websites offer not only material produced in-house (such as databases that serve as indexes to documents), but also images of documents housed elsewhere. Consequently, *some citations to a website may require only one layer* (as in Template 1), *while citations to other databases offered by that same website may require multiple layers.* (Template 5) As with all matters related to research, we must analyze each situation and use our judgment.

- *Public artifacts that are standalone objects,* such as grave markers in a cemetery, can be cited in one layer (Template 14), if we view the original stone and capture its information ourselves. If we use online images or transcripts, multiple layers are needed.

Within this framework, multiple sources can be cited within the same reference note. We simply place a period at the end of our citation to each published work, thereby ending that "citation sentence." Then we begin a new sentence for the next source.

To ensure clarity, Evidence Style does not cite multiple sources *within the same citation sentence.* (Within the same reference note, yes. Within the same sentence, no.)

Multi-layer Citations

History's emphasis upon using original documents as the basis for reliable research means that many citations need multiple layers. The content of those layers is dictated by how we access the materials: physically or online.

PHYSICAL ACCESS

Citations to *manuscript material* that we access in physical form require identification of three things:

- the document (*who, what, when,* and *where created*);
- the organizational scheme in which the document is archived (*where maintained*);
- the identity and location of that archives (*where accessed*).

Details for each of these three entities should be grouped in its own layer. As demonstrated in the bulleted lists above and below, that layer will often have internal commas and other punctuation. Thus, a semicolon is used between layers for a clear separation.

A full description of the document's location may also require us to subdivide the layer that details the organizational scheme, because

- formal archives typically hold documents within *files* or *boxes;*
- those files or boxes are part of a *collection;*
- each collection may be part of a *series;*
- each series may be part of a *record group.*

Each of these levels in the organizational scheme of an archive can have lengthy labels that require internal commas to separate names, descriptive details, and dates. For clear separation of each entity (document, file, collection, series, etc.), *each of these organizational levels is treated as a layer,* with a semicolon marking the division between one layer and the next.

ONLINE ACCESS

Online access to imaged documents requires the use of at least two layers and sometimes three:

- *Record Layer:* where we identify the original document, as fully as it can be identified *from the images themselves.*
- *Access Layer:* where we identify the website that delivers the images and (often) the specific database through which the images are accessed.
- *Location Layer (aka "Citing ..." Layer):* where we report the source information as given by the website—a layer we usually begin with the words "citing ..."

The "Citing ..." Layer is commonly used in one of two circumstances:

- *Database citations:* When Layer 1 presents all information from the database, including the item of interest, then the "Citing ..." Layer is used to report where the website or database says it obtained the information.

- *Online image citations:* Often those images, as filmed, do not completely document the original record. Sometimes, details needed to identify and locate the original source may appear only in the website's frame around the image, or in a sidebar, or in a separate source discussion. All of that is *background information created by the website*. It is not part of the original record. It is not information we can verify from the images themselves.

For these reasons, we add a layer to report that the *website* is "citing ... [thus and such]." We do not inject the website's information into the layer in which we cite what we actually see (and verify) in the images.

Sequence of Layers: Archived Records

When we cite original documents, the order of our building blocks may vary. These variations are not whimsical. They are shaped by the nature and organization of the material itself.

- *Authored and compiled manuscripts* (whether created by an individual, corporation, or government official) follow the same sequence we use for books: *Who, What, Where,* and *When,* followed by an internal location (*Where Within*) for the Specific Item. When done with that layer, we add a semicolon and begin the final layer to identify the office, agency, or private location where that material can be accessed. (Templates 6 and 9)

- *Manuscripts held by formal archives in the United States* call for citations that begin with the smallest element (typically *Who* and/or *What,* sometimes adding *Where, When*) and then progress to the largest element (the archive and its location). In other nations, that order may be reversed, starting with the largest element and working down to the smallest. When our research project spans multiple nations with differing conventions, consistency calls for choosing our native style. (Template 8)

Sequence of Layers: Online Images

For documents that are imaged online, citation layers might be described as mix-and-match. We select components and organize the layers as needed. Each layer is independent of the other. Each follows its own format, within two basic options:

EMPHASIS ON RECORD

This option is typically used when we have only one or a few documents from an online database. It creates a three-layer citation:

- *Layer 1* cites the imaged record, following the appropriate format for that type of document. (Templates 6–9)

- *Layer 2* cites the database and/or website, following the universal pattern for complex websites. (Template 5)

- *Layer 3* becomes the "Citing ..." Layer.

EMPHASIS ON DATABASE

This option is typically used when we have many items to cite from a single database. It normally requires just two layers:

- *Layer 1* cites the database and website, following the universal pattern for complex websites. (Template 5) Within this format, all the *Who, What, Where, When* information for the record itself is placed within the Specific Item Block.

- *Layer 2* becomes the "Citing ..." Layer.

The Rule That Has No Exception

The mix-and-match nature of citations to online images has one cardinal rule: *Details that describe one entity must not be assigned to a different entity.* Think of this as a Velcro Principle for online citations: what's meant to stick together should stick together.

If we choose Emphasis on Record, then all image details we use to identify the original record stay together in Layer 1, while all details that identify the website or database stay in Layer 2. For example:

- An imaged page may display an original *page* number, while the website's frame around that image may state an *image* number. The number of the image created by the website should not appear in the layer in which we cite the original document. Conversely, a page number used in an original record book would not be cited in the layer in which we identify the website.

- The title of the *website's database* can never be substituted for the *record title* in the layer that identifies the record. Any user's effort to find that database title within the original record set would fail, because the website's database title will not exist within the original record set.

*If we choose **Emphasis on Database**,* the image number is the first piece of information within the Specific Item Block. After stating the image number, we identify what appears on that image. All information about the imaged record appears together at this spot.

$\int$

How we assemble building blocks and layers depends upon whether a source is published or unpublished.

Published Materials

Published materials, whether printed or online, can follow one simple format that is easily adapted for both print and virtual media.

Basic Format: Publications
1. Author, *Title,* descriptor if needed (Publication Place: Publisher, year), page or figure, etc.

Templates 1–5 in the next chapter demonstrate how to adapt this Basic Format for the common forms of published materials.

- Template 1:   Basic Publication (Book or Simple Website)
- Template 2:   Book with Parts by Different Authors
- Template 3:   Journal or Magazine Article
- Template 4:   Newspaper Article
- Template 5:   Complex Website (Multiple Articles, Databases & AI Tools)

Unpublished Manuscripts & Artifacts

The structure of a citation to unpublished material significantly differs from the formats used for published material in three ways:

- ***Quotation marks vs. italics:*** Titles of unpublished materials, when titles exist, are placed in quotation marks. They are never italicized. Italics are used only for the titles of standalone publications.

- **Publication data:** For unpublished works, these details are replaced by creation data.

- **Access data:** The physical location of a source is essential for unpublished materials, while access locations are rarely cited for print-published works.

Beyond these three basics, the *structure* of citations to unpublished material is significantly different because (*a*) far more details are needed to identify and locate unpublished items; and (*b*) different types of facilities organize their materials in different ways.

Unpublished materials used for historical research are typically held as one of three types:

- **Privately held items:** These are most often inherited or gifted artifacts, including document copies shared by other researchers. (Template 7)

- **Archive and library collections:** Here, the scope and size of the collections dictate a formal and usually complex organizational system. Typically, these arrangements are found in academic, state, and national archives. (Template 8)

- **Agency records:** Usually created by local government or religious entities, these materials are relatively limited in scope and, consequently, organized more simply. (Template 9)

Documents held in formal archives and libraries are frequently maintained within a *layered* hierarchy that begins with a document and progresses to files, then boxes or bound registers, then collections, then series, then record groups.

Each layer of this hierarchy may carry a lengthy name or label and sometimes a number. Often that label carries a date or a date range that must be cited, not only for the material to be understood but also for it to be located. To ensure clarity in this string of labels that are often similarly named and dated, four punctuation conventions are common:

- *Commas* separate most details within a layer.
- *Parentheses* are usually used to group publication details.
- *Colons* are used to separate two pieces of paired details, as in a register's VOLUME: PAGE or a record group NUMBER: NAME.
- *Semicolons* separate the layers of a citation.

The resulting citation will be lengthy. That is unavoidable. Efforts to eliminate parts of the citation usually result in insufficient information for analysis or relocation. This is a point most researchers learn the hard way.

Stripped to bare essentials, all citations to unpublished materials will be adaptations of one basic pattern:

Basic Format: Unpublished Works

1. Author, "Title," descriptor if needed, place and time created; archival identifiers, as needed; Repository Name, City, State.

Citations to unpublished materials do not include the Publisher Block because they have not been published.

Templates 6–11 demonstrate how to adapt this Basic Format for the common forms of unpublished materials.

- Template 6: Basic Authored Manuscript
- Template 7: Private Holdings (Artifact or Manuscript Document)
- Template 8: Formal Archives (Artifact or Manuscript Document)
- Template 9: Government, Church, or Corporate Office (Record Book vs. Loose File)
- Template 10: Online Image (Named Database vs. No Named Database)
- Template 11: Preservation Microfilm

Stripped Bare Guide

Templates 12–14 cover three types of records for which unique constructions are needed:

- Template 12: Birth or Death Certificate (Not a Family Artifact)
- Template 13: Census
  (Online Image vs. Preservation Microfilm)
- Template 14: Gravestone (Viewed Personally)

Universal Templates

As new researchers, we crave *templates.* We want explicit formats for citations. We want formats we can follow in every jot and tittle. After all, if we copy some format exactly, our citations will always be perfect, *right?* Wrong!

Across written history, sources have been created in endless ways, by people in different cultures, with different ways of thinking. Recording styles vary, content varies, and—in the digital world—innovation constantly alters access and delivery. No rigid formula can cover the citation of every type of record. As researchers, we must always *think for ourselves*—analyzing our sources to identify the elements essential to relocation and evaluation of quality.

The templates used for Evidence Style citations are *examples,* not formulas. They are designed to be flexible. Whatever source you find, from any corner of the world, should be compatible with one of these templates. The mix-and-match nature of the building blocks and layers we learned in the preceding chapter will let you select the pieces of information relevant to that source and arrange them in a way that is thorough and understandable.

Template 1
Basic Publication (Book)

BUILDING BLOCK	EXAMPLE
1. Author/Creator	Joan DeJean
2. Title	*Mutinous Women: How French Convicts Became Founding Mothers of the Gulf Coast*
3. Descriptor	{not needed for this book}
4. Place (of publication)	New York
5. Publisher	Basic Books, Hatchett Book Group
6. Date	2022
7. Specific Item	page 123

Citation Sentences

First Reference Note:

1. Joan DeJean, *Mutinous Women: How French Convicts Became Founding Mothers of the Gulf Coast* (New York: Basic Books, Hatchett Book Group, 2022), 123.

Subsequent Reference Note:

11. DeJean, *Mutinous Women,* 123.

Source List Entry:

DeJean, Joan. *Mutinous Women: How French Convicts Became Founding Mothers of the Gulf Coast.* New York: Basic Books, Hatchett Book Group, 2022.

Construction Note

The formatting of reference notes and source list entries differ in three ways:
- Author's name is reversed in alphabetized source list entries, so that alphabetization will be by surname.
- Periods separate each element within a source list entry, while reference notes use periods only at the end of a citation sentence.
- Hanging-indent style is used in a source list entry, so the name or word used for alphabetizing is more easily spotted.

Template 1
Basic Publication (Simple Website)

BUILDING BLOCK	EXAMPLE
1. Author/creator	Lawrence Kestenbaum
2. Title	*The Political Graveyard: A Database of American History*
3. Descriptor	{not needed; the title is sufficiently descriptive}
4. Place (of pub. = URL)	https://www.politicalgraveyard.com
5. Publisher	{rarely needed for websites}
6. Date	accessed 1 January 2025
7. Specific Item	"Lucas Lugers"

Citation Sentences

First Reference Note:

1. Lawrence Kestenbaum, *The Political Graveyard: A Database of American History* (https://www.politicalgraveyard.com : accessed 1 January 2025), "Lucas Lugers."

Subsequent Reference Note:

11. Kestenbaum, *The Political Graveyard*, "Lucas Lugers."

Source List Entry:

Kestenbaum, Lawrence. *The Political Graveyard: A Database of American History.* https://www.politicalgraveyard.com : 1 January 2025.

Construction Note

The format for a simple website is the same as that for a standard book (facing page). Both are basic publications that need the same pieces of information to identify them.

For websites offering image generators, large language models, and other artificial intelligence tools, use Template 5: Complex Websites.

Stripped Bare Guide

Template 2
Book with Parts by Different Authors
Adapted from Template 1: Basic Publication

BUILDING BLOCK	EXAMPLE
1. Author/Creator (of chapter)	Marvin D. Jeter
2. Title (of chapter)	"Ripe for Colonial Exploitation: Ancient Traditions of Violence and Enmity as Preludes to the Indian Slave Trade"
1. Editor/Creator (of book)	Max Carocci and Stephanie Pratt, editors
2. Title (of book)	*Native American Adoption, Captivity, and Slavery in Changing Contexts*
3. Descriptor	{none needed in this case}
4. Place (of publication)	New York
5. Publisher	Palgrave Macmillan
6. Date	2012
7. Specific Item	pages 23–46, specifically 31

Citation Sentences

First Reference Note:

1. Marvin D. Jeter, "Ripe for Colonial Exploitation: Ancient Traditions of Violence and Enmity as Preludes to the Indian Slave Trade," Max Carocci and Stephanie Pratt, editors, *Native American Adoption, Captivity, and Slavery in Changing Contexts* (New York: Palgrave Macmillan, 2012), 23–46, specifically 31.

Subsequent Reference Note:

11. Jeter, "Ripe for Colonial Exploitation," 31.

Source List Entry:

Jeter, Marvin D. "Ripe for Colonial Exploitation: Ancient Traditions of Violence and Enmity as Preludes to the Indian Slave Trade." Max Carocci and Stephanie Pratt, editors. *Native American Adoption, Captivity, and Slavery in Changing Contexts*. New York: Palgrave Macmillan, 2012.

Template 3
Journal or Magazine Article
Adapted from Template 1: Basic Publication

BUILDING BLOCK	EXAMPLE
1. Author/Creator	Elizabeth Shown Mills
2. Title (of article)	"Laying a Legend to Rest: Marie Thérèse Coincoin and Archaeological Sites 16NA785 and 16NA789"
1. Editor/Creator	{not used for journals or magazines}
2. Title (of journal)	*Louisiana History*
3. Descriptor	volume 62
4. Place (of publication)	{not used for print works; cite URL for online works}
5. Publisher	{not used for journals or magazines}
6. Date	Summer 2021
7. Specific Item	177–224, specifically Map 1

Citation Sentences

First Reference Note:

    1. Elizabeth Shown Mills, "Laying a Legend to Rest: Marie Thérèse Coincoin and Archaeological Sites 16NA785 and 16NA789," *Louisiana History* 62 (Summer 2021): 177–224, specifically Map 1.

Subsequent Reference Note:

    11. Mills, "Laying a Legend to Rest," 178.

Source List Entry:

Mills, Elizabeth Shown. "Laying a Legend to Rest: Marie Thérèse Coincoin and Archaeological Sites 16NA785 and 16NA789." *Louisiana History* 62 (Summer 2021): 177–224.

Template 4
Newspaper Article
Adapted from Template 1: Basic Publication

BUILDING BLOCK	EXAMPLE
1. Author/Creator	[no author named]
2. Title (of article)	"A Rally for the Union"
2. Title (of newspaper)	*Natchez Daily Courier*
3. Descriptor	{not needed in this case}
4. Place (of publication)	Natchez, Mississippi
5. Publisher	{not used for newspapers}
6. Date	17 September 1850
7. Specific Item	page 2, columns 4–5

Citation Sentences

First Reference Note:

1. "A Rally for the Union," *Natchez* [Mississippi] *Daily Courier,* 17 September 1850, page 2, columns 4–5.

Subsequent Reference Note:

11. "A Rally for the Union," col. 5.

Source List Entry:

"A Rally for the Union." *Natchez* [Mississippi] *Daily Courier,* 17 September 1850.

(or, if you examine a whole run of issues)
Natchez [Mississippi] *Daily Courier.* 1845–1857.

Template 5
Complex Website (Multiple Articles, Databases & AI Tools)
Adapted from Template 2: Book with Parts by Different Authors

BUILDING BLOCK	EXAMPLE
1. Author/Creator (of database)	Gwendolyn Midlo Hall
2. Title	"Louisiana, U.S., Slave Manumission Records, 1719–1820"
3. Descriptor	database without images
1. Creator (website)	{not needed for this website}
2. Title	*Ancestry*
4. Place (pub.) = URL 5. Publisher 6. Date	https://www.ancestry.com/search/collections/7382/ {accessed 1 January 2025
7. Specific Item	search term: "Augustin Metoyer," entry "Dorothee"
3. Descriptor (when needed)	citing "Hall, *Afro-History and Genealogy, 1719–1820,* ibiblio.org/laslave"

Citation Sentences

First Reference Note

    1. "Lousiana, U.S., Slave Manumission Records, 1719–1820," database, *Ancestry* (https://www.ancestry.com/search/collections /7382/ : accessed 1 January 2025), search term: "Augustin Metoyer," entry for "Dorothee"; **citing "Hall, Afro-History and Genealogy, 1719–1820, ibiblio.org/laslave."**

Subsequent Reference Note

    11. "Lousiana, U.S., Slave Manumission Records, 1719–1820," search term: "Augustin Metoyer," entry for "Dorothee."

Source List Entry:

"Lousiana, U.S., Slave Manumission Records, 1719–1820." Database. *Ancestry.* https://www.ancestry.com/search/collections /7382/ : 1 January 2025.

Construction Note

Shading denotes an added layer. Layer 1 cites the source (the database). Layer 2 reports where the source says it obtained its information.

Template 6
Basic Authored Manuscript

BUILDING BLOCK	EXAMPLE
1. Author/Creator	Jacob Brightstar
2. Title	"Home in the Choctaw Diaspora: Survival and Remembrance Away from Nanih Waiya"
3. Descriptor	Thesis
4. Place (of creation) 5. Publisher 6. Date (of creation)	University of Kansas {not used for a manuscript} 2022
7. Specific Item	page 123
4. Place (of access)	University of Kansas Library, Lawrence

Citation Sentences

First Reference Note:

1. Jacob Brightstar, "Home in the Choctaw Diaspora: Survival and Remembrance Away from Nanih Waiya," thesis (University of Kansas: 2022), 123; **held by University of Kansas Library, Lawrence.**

Subsequent Reference Note:

11. Brightstar, "Home in the Choctaw Diaspora," 123.

Source List Entry:

Brightstar, Jacob. "Home in the Choctaw Diaspora: Survival and Remembrance Away from Nanih Waiya." Thesis. University of Kansas: 2022. University of Kansas Library, Lawrence.

Construction Note

Shading defines the layers.

Template 6, above, has two layers. Its Layer 1 cites the source (the thesis). Layer 2 reports where the thesis is located.

Template 7, at right, has three layers. Its Layer 1 identifies the source (the letter). Layer 2 reports where the letter is located. Layer 3 provides provenance needed to support authenticity.

Template 7
Private Holdings (Artifact or Manuscript Document)

BUILDING BLOCK	EXAMPLE
1. Author/Creator	F. A. Charleville to "Dear Sister" [Athanaïse Charleville Faris]
2. Title/label	{none in this case}
3. Descriptor	letter
4. Place (of creation) 6. Date (of creation)	Fiddletown, California 15 November 1867
7. Specific Item	page 2
4. Place (of access)	Mills Family Papers, 1850–, privately held by E.S. Mills, [ADDRESS FOR PRIVATE USE,] Hendersonville, Tennessee
5. Date/year (of access)	2025
3. Descriptor (provenance)	A descendant of Athanaïse gave the inherited letter to F. A. Charleville's great-grandson, Charles King of Oakland, California, who passed it to Mills in 1972.

Citation Sentences

First Reference Note:

1. F. A. Charleville to "Dear Sister" [Athanaïse Charleville Faris], letter, California, 15 November 1867; **Mills Family Papers, 1850–, privately held by E. S. Mills, [ADDRESS FOR PRIVATE USE,] Hendersonville, Tennessee, 2025.** A descendant of Athanaïse gave the inherited letter to F. A. Charleville's great-grandson, Charles King of Oakland, California, who passed it to Mills in 1972.

Subsequent Note:

11. F. A. Charleville to "Dear Sister," letter, California, 15 Nov. 1867.

Source List Entry:

Charleville, F. A. To "Dear Sister" [Athanaïse Charleville Faris]. Letter. California. 15 November 1867. Mills Family Papers, 1850–, privately held by E. S. Mills, [ADDRESS FOR PRIVATE USE,] Hendersonville, Tennessee, 2025. A descendant of Athanaïse gave the inherited letter to F. A. Charleville's great-grandson, Charles King of Oakland, California, who passed it to Mills in 1972.

Template 8
Formal Archives (Artifact or Manuscript Document)

BUILDING BLOCK	EXAMPLE
1. Author/Creator (if needed)	Franklin County, Virginia
2. Title/label	"List of Insolvent lands in the county of Franklin for the year 1790"
6. Date	filed November Court 1792
3. Descriptor	semi-alphabetized
7. Specific Item	entries for Richard and James Edmondson
1. Title (of folder)	"Franklin County Delinquent & Insolvent Lists, 1790–1813"
2. Title (of collection)	accession no. 23707: Franklin County Tax and Fiscal Records
4. Place (of access)	Library of Virginia, Richmond

Citation Sentences

First Reference Note:

1. Franklin County, Virginia, "List of Insolvent lands in the county of Franklin for the year 1790," filed November Court 1792, semi-alphabetized, entries for Richard and James Edmondson; **folder: "Franklin County Delinquent & Insolvent Lists, 1790–1813"**; accession no. 23707: Franklin County Tax and Fiscal Records; **Library of Virginia, Richmond.**

Subsequent Reference Note:

11. Franklin Co., Va., "List of Insolvent lands in the county of Franklin for the year 1790," entries for Richard and James Edmondson.

Source List Entry:

Franklin Co., Va. "List of Insolvent lands in the county of Franklin for the year 1790." Filed November Court 1792. Folder: "Franklin County Delinquent & Insolvent Lists, 1790–1813." Accession no. 23707: Franklin County Tax and Fiscal Records. Library of Virginia, Richmond.

Template 8
Construction Notes:

The organization of records within formal archives differs significantly from the simpler organization used for local government offices, churches, and other agencies (Template 9).

Documents kept in formal archives can require numerous layers to identify the organizational scheme by which they are found. This document requires four layers: (*a*) the document; (*b*) the named folder; (*c*) the named collection; and (*d*) the repository and its city where the document may be accessed.

Layer 1:
- **Author/Creator.** The creator of tax rolls for a county or city will be the county or city—not the employee who compiled the rolls.
- **Document title.** When a document carries a formal title, its title is copied exactly, with quotation marks.
- **Date.** The document is undated. We are told only that it was filed in the November Term of Court, 1792. Thus, that court term is cited as its date of creation.
- **Persons of interest.** These are named in the Specific Item field.

Layer 2:
- **Author/Creator.** There is no additional creator at the archival level.
- **Title (folder).** The folder in which the archive holds this document carries a specific label. All words are copied exactly, with quotation marks around the quoted words. They are specifically identified as the title of the *folder* so that set of identifying words will not be confused with the title of the *document* or the title of the *collection.*

Layer 3:
- **Title (collection).** The archives has assigned both a name and an accession number to this collection. The accession number (or record group number, when the archival hierarchy calls for identification of a record group) is cited *before* the collection name, with the two separated by a colon. Collection titles created by archives are not placed in quotation marks, but the words should be copied exactly.

Layer 4:
- **Place.** Here we identify the repository that maintains this record and the location of that repository. When the state's identity is part of the repository name, then the state name does not have to be repeated again after the identification of city.

Stripped Bare Guide

Template 9
Government, Church, or Corporate Office (Record Book)

BUILDING BLOCK	EXAMPLE
1. Author/Creator	Big Horn County, Wyoming
2. Title	Untitled miscellaneous record book, 1897–1900
3. Descriptor (for title)	{no further descriptor needed for this particular title}
7. Specific Item	page 41
3. Descriptor (for specific item)	A. L. Pease mining affidavit
6. Date	17 July 1897
4. Place (of access)	County Clerk's Office, Cheyenne

Citation Sentences

First Reference Note:

1. Big Horn County, Wyoming, Untitled miscellaneous record book, 1897–1900, page 41, A. L. Pease mining affidavit, 17 July 1897; **County Clerk's Office, Cheyenne.**

Subsequent Reference Note:

11. Big Horn Co., Wyo., Untitled miscellaneous record book, 1897–1900, p. 41.

Source List Entry

Big Horn County, Wyoming. Untitled miscellaneous record book, 1897–1900. County Clerk's Office, Cheyenne.

(or)

Wyoming, Big Horn County. Untitled miscellaneous record book, 1897–1900. County Clerk's Office, Cheyenne.

Construction Note

Shading denotes an added layer. Layer 1 cites the source (the county register). Layer 2 reports where the source is located.

Template 9
Government, Church, or Corporate Office (Loose File)

BUILDING BLOCK	EXAMPLE
1. Creator (of file)	Obion County, Tennessee
2. Title/label (of series)	Circuit Court Files
2. Title/label (of file)	case no. 1335: Nancy Covington vs. Ed Covington
3. Descriptor (for file)	petition by Nancy, 2 pp.
7. Specific Item	page 1
6. Date (of document)	29 November 1861
4. Place (of access)	Circuit Court Clerk's Office, Union City

Citation Sentences

First Reference Note:

1. Obion County, Tennessee, Circuit Court case no. 135: Nancy Covington vs. Ed Covington, petition by Nancy, 2 pp., 29 November 1861; **Circuit Court Clerk's Office, Union City.**

Subsequent Reference Note:

11. Obion Co., Tenn., Circuit Court case no. 135: Nancy Covington vs. Ed Covington, petition by Nancy, 29 Nov. 1861.

Source List Entry:

Obion County, Tennessee. Circuit Court Files. 1861. Circuit Court Clerk's Office, Union City.

(or)

Tennessee, Obion County. Circuit Court Files. 1861. Circuit Court Clerk's Office, Union City.

Construction Note

Shading denotes an added layer. Layer 1 cites the source (the court files). Layer 2 reports where the source is located.

Template 10
Online Image (Named Database)
Combining Templates 9: Government Office *and* 5: Complex Website

BUILDING BLOCK	EXAMPLE
1. Author/Creator	Christian County, Kentucky
2. Title	Will Book A
3. Descriptor	{not needed for this register}
7. Specific Item	pages 46–47
3. Descriptor (specific item)	Thomas Wadlington estate inventory
6. Date (specific item)	undated, filed December 1803
Bridge words between document and website provider	imaged,
1. Creator	{not needed for self-named site}
2. Title (of database, if any)	"Kentucky Probate Records, 1727–1990"
2. Title (of website)	*FamilySearch*
4. Place (of pub. = URL) 6. Date	https://www.familysearch.org/search/collection/1875188 accessed 1 January 2025
7. Specific Item (including the path)	Christian > Will Records Index 1797–1811, Vol. A > images 35–36 of 137
3. Descriptor (website's source)	citing "county courthouses, Kentucky"

Citation Sentences

First Reference Note:
1. Christian County, Kentucky, Will Book A: 46–47, Thomas Wadlington estate inventory, undated, filed December 1803; **imaged, "Kentucky Probate Records, 1727–1990,"** *FamilySearch* **(https://www.familysearch.org/search/collection/1875188 : accessed 1 January 2025) > Christian > Will Records Index 1797–1811, Vol. A > images 35–36 of 137**; citing "county courthouses, Kentucky."

Subsequent Reference Note:
11. Christian Co. Ky., Will Book A: 46–47.

Source List Entry:
Christian County, Kentucky. Will Book A. Imaged. "Kentucky Probate Records, 1727–1990." *FamilySearch.* https://www.familysearch.org/search/collection/1875188 : 2025.

Template 10
Online Image (No Named Database)
Combining Templates 9: Government Office *and* 5: Complex Website

BUILDING BLOCK	EXAMPLE
1. Author/Creator	Billings County, North Dakota
2. Title	Naturalization Records 1890 to 1912
3. Descriptor	volume 1
7. Specific Item	page 25
3. Descriptor (specific item)	Hans Erlandson, declaration of intention
6. Date (specific item)	26 September 1898
Bridge words between document and website provider	imaged,
1. Creator	{not needed for self-named site}
2. Title (of website)	*FamilySearch*
4. Place (of pub.) = URL 6. Date	https://www.familysearch.org accessed 1 January 2025
7. Specific Item (film ID)	image group number 7785260 > image 24 of 689
3. Descriptor (website's source)	citing "State Historical Society, Bismarck, N.D."

Citation Sentences

First Reference Note:

1. Billings County, North Dakota, Naturalization Records 1890 to 1912, volume 1, page 25, Hans Erlandson, declaration of intention, 26 September 1898; imaged, *FamilySearch* (https://www.familysearch .org : accessed 1 January 2025) > image group number (IGN) 7785260 > image 24 of 689; citing "State Historical Society, Bismarck."

Subsequent Reference Note:

11. Billings Co., N.D., Naturalization Records 1890 to 1912, vol. 1, p. 25.

Source List Entry:

Billings County, North Dakota. Naturalization Records 1890 to 1912. Imaged. *FamilySearch*. https://www.familysearch.org : 2025. Image group number (IGN) 7785260.

Template 11
Preservation Microfilm

Adapted from Template 9: Government, Church, or Corporate Office

BUILDING BLOCK	EXAMPLE
1. Author/Creator	Uxbridge Monthly Meeting (Uxbridge, Massachusetts)
2. Title	"Book of Records for Epistles, Certificates, Testimonies of Denial and Acknowledgements"
3. Descriptor (for title)	1783–1811
7. Specific Item	page 24
3. Descriptor (for item)	Disownment of Enoch Philipps
6. Date	December 1781
Bridge words bet. document and web provider	imaged,
2. Title or ID of film	FSL microfilm 1324 > item 3
4. Place (of access) 6. Date	FamilySearch Library, Salt Lake City {date of filming not shown; date of access not needed because film does not change}
7. Specific Item	{no frame number shown on film}
3. Descriptor (website's source)	citing "Friends Historical Library, Swarthmore, Pennsylvania"

Citation Sentences

First Reference Note:

1. Uxbridge Monthly Meeting (Uxbridge, Massachusetts), "Book of Records for Epistles, Certificates, Testimonies of Denial and Acknowledgements," 1783–1811, page 24, disownment of Enoch Philipps, December 1781; **imaged, FSL microfilm 1324 > item 3, Family Search Library, Salt Lake City**; citing "Friends Historical Library, Swarthmore, Pennsylvania."

Subsequent Reference Note:

11. Uxbridge Monthly Meeting, "Book of Records for Epistles, Certificates, [Etc.]," 1783–1811, p. 24.

Source List Entry:

Uxbridge Monthly Meeting (Uxbridge, Massachusetts). "Book of Records for Epistles, Certificates, Testimonies of Denial and Acknowledgements," 1783–1811. Imaged. FSL microfilm 1324 > item 3. Family Search Library, Salt Lake City, Utah.

Template 12
Birth or Death Certificate
(Not a family artifact)

BUILDING BLOCK	EXAMPLE
1. Creator (of document)	Ohio, Division of Vital Statistics
2. Title/label (of document)	Certificate of Death
7. Specific Item • Certificate no. (year) • County reporting event • Person • Date of event	 no. 21728 (1931) Atkens County Margaret E. Davis died 20 April 1931
6. Date	issued 4 April 2021
4. Person (issued to)	John Erl [ADDRESS FOR PRIVATE USE], Lima, Ohio

Citation Sentences

First Reference Note:

1. Ohio, Division of Vital Statistics, Certificate of Death no. 21728 (1931), Atkens County, Margaret E. Davis, died 20 April 1931; **issued 4 April 2021 to John Erl,** [ADDRESS FOR PRIVATE USE,] **Lima, Ohio.**

Subsequent Reference Note:

11. Ohio, Certificate of Death no. 21728 (1931), Atkens County, Margaret E. Davis, died 20 April 1931.

Source List Entry:

Ohio. Division of Vital Statistics. Certificate of Death no. 21728 (1931), Atkens County. Margaret E. Davis, died 20 April 1931. Issued 4 April 2021 to John Erl, [ADDRESS FOR PRIVATE USE,] Lima, Ohio.

(or, when many certificates were obtained)
Ohio. Division of Vital Statistics. Death Certificates.

Template 13
Census (Online Image)

Combining Basic Format: Unpublished Works
and Template 5: Complex Website

BUILDING BLOCK	EXAMPLE
1. Author/Creator	United States (U.S.)
2. Title	1850 census
4. Place (of creation) 6. Date (of creation)	Marion County, Iowa {year of census appears in "descriptive title"}
3. Descriptor	population schedule
7. Specific Item	Lake Prairie, page 290 (stamped), dwelling 151, family 156, Virgil W. and Wyatt B. Earp
Bridge words between document & website provider	imaged,
1. Creator	{not needed for self-named site}
2. Title (of database)	"1850 United States Federal Census"
2. Title (of website)	*Ancestry*
4. Place of pub. = URL 6. Date	https://www.ancestry.com/search/collections/8054/ : accessed 1 January 2025
7. Specific Item	{may or may not be needed}
3. Descriptor (website's source)	{may or may not be needed}

Citation Sentences
First Reference Note:

1. U.S. 1850 census [OR 1850 U.S. census], Marion County, Iowa, population schedule, Lake Prairie, page 290 (stamped), dwelling 151, family 156, Virgil W. and Wyatt B. Earp; **imaged in "1850 United States Federal Census,"** *Ancestry* **(https://www.ancestry.com/search/collec tions/8054 : accessed 1 January 2025).**

Subsequent Reference Note:

11. U.S. 1850 census, Marion Co., Ia., pop. sch., Lake Prairie, p. 290 (stamped), dwell.151, fam.156, Virgil W. and Wyatt B. Earp.

Source List Entry

U.S. 1850 census. Marion County, Iowa. Population schedule. Imaged. "1850 United States Federal Census." *Ancestry.* https://www.ancestry .com/search/collections/8054 : 2025.

Template 13
Census (Preservation Microfilm)
Combining Basic Format: Unpublished Works
and Template 11: Preservation Microfilm

BUILDING BLOCK	EXAMPLE
1. Author/Creator	United States (U.S.)
2. Title	1850 census
4. Place (of creation) 6. Date (of creation)	Hinds County, Mississippi {year of census appears in "descriptive title"}
3. Descriptor	population schedule (state-level copy)
7. Specific Item	page 21, dwelling 156, family 156, James B. Smylie
Bridge words	imaged,
1. Creator	{in-house film; no need to cite a creator}
2. Title or ID of film	MDAH microfilm 2528
4. Place (of access) 6. Date	Mississippi Department of Archives and History, Jackson {date of filming not shown; date of access not needed because film is fixed; it does not change}
7. Specific Item	{no frame number shown on film}
3. Descriptor (website's source)	citing series 102, Secretary of State Papers

Citation Sentences
First Reference Note:

1. U.S. 1850 census [OR 1850 U.S. census], Hinds County, Mississippi, population schedule (state-level copy), page 21, dwelling 156, family 156, James B. Smylie; **imaged, MDAH microfilm 2528, Mississippi Department of Archives and History, Jackson**; citing series 102, Secretary of State Papers.

First Reference Note:

11. U.S. 1850 census, Hinds Co., Miss., pop, sch. (state-level copy), p. 21, dwell.156, fam.156, James B. Smylie.

Source List Entry

U.S. 1850 census. Hinds County, Mississippi. Population schedule (state-level copy). Imaged. MDAH microfilm 2528. Mississippi Department of Archives and History, Jackson.

Stripped Bare Guide

Template 14
Gravestone (Viewed Personally)

BUILDING BLOCK	EXAMPLE
1. Author/Creator	Waldheim Cemetery (Forest Park, Cook County, Illinois)
2. Title	{not applicable}
3. Descriptor	{not applicable}
4. Place (of access)	1400 Des Plaines Avenue
7. Specific Item	Egbert Petersen marker, section 555C
3. Descriptor	personally read
6. Date	2022

Citation Sentences

First Reference Note:

1. Waldheim Cemetery (Forest Park, Cook County, Illinois), 1400 Des Plaines Avenue, Egbert Petersen marker, section 555C, personally read, 2022.

Subsequent Reference Note:

11. Waldheim Cemetery, Egbert Petersen marker, section 555C.

Source List Entry:

Waldheim Cemetery (Forest Park, Cook County, Illinois). 1400 Des Plaines Avenue. Egbert Petersen marker, section 555C.

Template 14
Construction Notes

The following special guidelines exist for citing cemeteries that we personally visit:

- **Author/creator.** The agency that operates the cemetery is cited as the creator. Its location (City, County, State or Province) should be added, in parentheses, as part of the Creator's identity.

- **Date.** The date cited will be the date the reading was made, not a date from the stone. The date carved on the stone will be part of our research notes, not our source note.

- **Descriptor.** As additional items in this field, we may note the condition of the marker, the material from which it is made, and whether or not that material and the marker's style is contemporary with the dates on the marker. All of these details address the question *Why should I believe the information I am taking from this source?*

- **Layers.** A citation to a cemetery or monument that we personally visit does not require multiple layers.

- **Place.** At least three common methods exist for identifying the place where a grave marker is found: (1) GPS coordinates; (2) street/road/highway address; and (3) the Township-Range-Section and fraction designations in rural areas. You should choose the most appropriate method for each situation.

(Online gravestone data)

When we cite tombstone images we have found online, or tombstone data without images, *we are not citing the tombstone and graveyard.* We are citing a website and database. (See Template 5) If an image is attached to a memorial page, it is identified in the Specific Item Block. If only an extraction exists—or only a memorial page—then we identify it as such, name the contributor, and note that no image or evidence is provided.

Our "Citing ..." Layer will report the identity of the cemetery as cited by the website.

The distinction here is significant: When citing online images of a stone, or tombstone data, we cannot vouch for the authenticity of the image or the accuracy of the data—as we can when citing our personal observation made amid an onsite visit.

Appendixes

Appendix 1: Glossary

abstract: (academic context) a brief summary or précis of principal points in an essay or a thesis.

abstract: (notetaking context) a condensed version of a record, preserving all important detail in original sequence. An abstract may contain verbatim quotes of passages from the record—i.e., *extracts* (q.v.)—in which case the material that is copied exactly should be placed in quotation marks inside the abstract.

acronym: a "word" coined by combining the initial letter of each word that identifies an institution, a law, etc. Example: NARA, as a short form for National Archives and Records Administration. Compare to *initialism* (q.v.)

analysis: the process of examining evidence. For students of history, this typically involves (*a*) studying individual pieces of data for inherent clues, strengths, and weaknesses; (*b*) correlating details from different sources in search of patterns and contradictions; and (*c*) determining whether the whole body of evidence amounts to more than the sum of the parts.

assertion: a claim or purported "fact"; it is only as valid as the evidence presented to support it.

assumption: a conclusion unsupported by evidence.

attested copy: (legal context) a copy of an original that has been officially compared to the original and attested to be a true copy (q.v. *examined copy*).

authored work: a new and original narrative; in historical research, typically a work created by someone who studies many records and the relevant works of other authors, drawing from this study a synthesis of knowledge on the subject and a set of personal conclusions. An *authored* work is not to be confused with a *compiled work* (q.v.).

best evidence: an original record or records of the best and highest quality that survives. At law and in history research, a *derivative source* (q.v.) is rarely considered sufficient for documentation when an original (or a derivative closer to the original) exists.

beyond reasonable doubt: a legal standard applied in criminal cases, requiring virtual certainty; rarely appropriate for history research.

bibliography: a list of sources relevant to the subject at hand. An *annotated* bibliography is one that discusses the sources in addition to providing full citations. A bibliography typically does not cite individual manuscripts or documents; rather, it cites a collection or series in which the manuscript appears. Also see *source list* (q.v.).

calendar: (archival context) a collection guide that contains brief descriptions of each item in that collection, sometimes arranged in chronological order.

circumstantial case: (historical context) a reasonable conclusion reached by assembling, analyzing, and explaining, with thorough documentation, numerous pieces of *indirect evidence* (q.v.).

circumstantial evidence: (legal context) testimony based on deductions drawn from various information that can be documented.

citation: a statement in which one identifies a source consulted or the source of a specific *assertion*. Common forms of citations are *source list entries* (bibliographic entries), *reference notes* (*endnotes* or *footnotes*), and *document labels* (q.v. all italicized terms).

citation sentence: the format used for *footnotes* and *endnotes* (q.v.), wherein all details identifying a source are expressed sentence-style, with a period placed only at the end. Compare to *source list entry* (q.v.), created paragraph style, wherein periods are placed between each element that identifies that source.

(to) cite: the act of identifying a source or sources that support an assertion, not to be confused with the homonyms *site* (as in *website*) or *sight* (as in *eyesight*).

claim: an assertion of "fact" for which no evidence is supplied or else the evidence is insufficient or has not yet been adjudged.

clear and convincing evidence: a legal standard interchangeable with *beyond reasonable doubt* (q.v.) in some regions; elsewhere, an intermediate standard between *beyond reasonable doubt* (q.v.) and *preponderance of the evidence* (q.v.); not a standard appropriate for historical research.

clerk's copy: a term typically used for the officially recorded copy of a document (q.v. *record copy*).

compiled work: an aggregation of data, abstracted records, and similar raw materials, presented without an effort to form analytical conclusions of the type that characterize an *authored work* (q.v.).

conclusion: a decision. To be reliable, it must be based on well-reasoned and thoroughly documented evidence gleaned from reasonably exhaustive research in the best surviving sources.

(to) confirm: to test the accuracy of an assertion or conclusion by (*a*) consulting other sources that are both independently created and authoritative; and (*b*) finding agreement or compatibility between them.

conflicting evidence: relevant pieces of information from disparate sources that contradict one another.

copyright: the exclusive right to copy, distribute, or license a creative work or to exploit it in any other manner. The term should not be rendered as *copywrite*. The issue at law is that of *rights*, not the act of *writing*.

(to) correlate: to compare and contrast separate items in order to identify associations, similarities, and dissimilarities.

correlation: an analytical comparison of disparate pieces of information to identify associations, similarities, and dissimilarities. Correlation of details should be conducted within each individual record and across all records found.

(to) corroborate: to *confirm* (q.v.).

credibility: believability, reliability; a quality that represents likely truth or reality; a state of acceptability earned by meeting standards for source quality, evidence analysis, and thorough research to assure that the document or the information does represent *best evidence* (q.v.).

deduction: a conclusion inferred from aggregated clues.

"definitive source": a false concept based on the presumption that a certain source is always reliable or represents the "final word" on an issue.

derivative source: material produced by copying an original document or manipulating its content. Abstracts, compendiums, compilations, databases, extracts, indexes, transcripts, and translations are all derivatives. Compare to *original record* (q.v.).

direct evidence: relevant information that explicitly states an answer to a research question or appears to solve a research problem all by itself. Compare to *indirect evidence* (q.v.).

discursive note: a reference note, keyed to text, that discusses tangential matters related in some way to the narrative but not directly on topic.

document—noun: (historical context) an official record; not to be confused with the technological usage wherein anything produced within software is called a "document." (legal context) any piece of writing submitted into evidence;

(to) document—verb: to provide credible *evidence* (q.v.) in the form of a *document* (q.v.) or a *proof argument* (q.v.) based on thorough research, credible evidence, and sound reasoning.

document label: a citation added to a loose document or photocopy, typically constructed in First Reference Note format.

duplicate original: a copy officially made at the same time as the actual original. Examples: a *letterpress copy book* (q.v.) of correspondence; or the grantor's and grantee's copies of a deed, simultaneously made; or the multiple copies of a census schedule that enumerators were required to submit in certain years.

edition: the version or form in which a publication is presented. It may be identified as an ordinal (e.g., first edition), as a descriptive term (e.g., revised edition, imaged edition), or in other media formats (e.g., CD-ROM edition, HTML edition, microfilm edition, online edition).

endnote: a *reference note* (q.v.) that is placed at the end of an essay, chapter, book, or other piece of writing. Compare to *footnote* (q.v.).

evidence: information or assertions that are relevant to the research question. Common forms used in historical analysis include *best evidence* (q.v.), *direct evidence* (q.v.), *indirect evidence* (q.v.), and *negative evidence* (q.v.). In a legal forum, the more generic *circumstantial evidence* (q.v.) is also common.

evidence books: record books maintained by some courts in which clerks have transcribed the evidence presented in cases before that court.

examined copy: an *attested copy* (q.v.).

exhibition copy: (census context) the copy that, in earlier times, was locally posted in public places or made available to the public for examination.

extract: a portion of text that is copied verbatim from a record and enclosed in quotation marks. An extract is more precise but less complete than an *abstract* (q.v.). Unlike a *transcript* (q.v.), it does not represent the complete record.

facsimile: an exact copy, usually a printed image copy.

fact: a presumed reality—an event, circumstance, or other detail that is considered to have happened or is widely accepted as true. In historical research, it is difficult to establish actual truths; therefore, the validity of any stated "fact" rests upon the quality of the *evidence* (q.v.) presented to support it.

factoid: a "fact" that is fictitious or unsubstantiated but repeatedly asserted to promote its acceptance.

"fair copy": a term used by the U.S. Census Bureau to describe the *duplicate original* (q.v.) that enumerators were required to submit in some years. Practically speaking, the term meant a "reasonably accurate" copy.

Fair Use Doctrine: an adjunct of copyright law, defining conditions under which one may use portions of copyrighted material for educational or informational purposes.

Stripped Bare Guide

First Reference Note: the first *citation* (q.v.) for a particular source, at which time the source is cited in full, with any descriptive detail or discussion needed for identification and analysis. Compare to *short-form citation* (q.v) and *Subsequent Reference Note* (q.v.).

folio: a large sheet of paper folded to make leaves or pages of a book or booklet—typically four pages or multiples of four. The term is also used for a single leaf of a historical manuscript in which only one side of the leaf is numbered.

footnote: a *reference note* (q.v.) placed at the bottom or foot of the page on which its corresponding text appears. Compare to *endnote* (q.v.).

FSL: the common initialism used for the FamilySearch Library system centered in Salt Lake City, Utah.

Genealogical Proof Standard (GPS): the genealogy field's standard of proof for reaching a conclusion about any "fact" or identity. Its five criteria are (*a*) reasonably exhaustive research in quality records, using all appropriate methodology; (*b*) thorough identification of each piece of evidence consulted; (*c*) correlation and analysis of evidence, individually and collectively; (*d*) a resolution of conflicting evidence; and (*e*) a written proof statement or argument that details both evidence and reasoning.

genealogy: the study of families in genetic and historical context; the study of communities in which kinship networks create the fabric of economic, political, and social life; the study of family structures and the changing roles of men, women, and children in diverse cultures; the study of biography, reconstructing individual human lives and placing them into family context across place and time. Otherwise, the study and story of who we are and how we came to be as individuals and societies.

hearsay: typically oral information of low evidentiary quality, being secondhand (secondary), thirdhand (tertiary), or otherwise not original. It may be handed down through the generations as "tradition" or passed around among contemporaries.

hypothesis: a proposition based upon an analysis of evidence at hand; not a *conclusion* (q.v.) but a premise used to focus research more narrowly in order to prove or disprove a possibility.

ibid.: an abbreviation for *ibidem,* meaning "in the same place (source) as the one cited immediately above." Within a *refer-*

ence note (q.v.), *ibid.* is used only when the preceding note cites just one source.

image copy: a digital, film, or photo image. In historical research, it is typically treated as an original, so long as no evidence suggests that the image may have been altered.

independent source: a source that did not take its information from any other. Researchers seek multiple independent, *original* sources (q.v. *original record*) to verify, correct, or disprove information.

indirect evidence: relevant information that does not directly answer the research question but can be used with other evidence to suggest an answer or build a conclusive case to answer the question. Compare to *direct evidence* (q.v.).

"indirect source": a term some writing guides use for the source from which a source obtained its information. Many careful researchers prefer "source of the source" for this concept. Because *source (q.v.)* and *evidence* (q.v.) are terms frequently confused, the term *indirect* is best used only with the word *evidence* and not with the term *source.*

inference: a deduction from information that implies something it does not state outright.

information: a statement or detail offered by a source. Information exists in three basic weights, *primary information* (q.v.), *secondary information* (q.v.), and unknown quality.

initialism: a coined "word" created by combining the initial letter(s) of several words to identify a thing, place, or concept. Initialisms are written in all capital letters (or, by the canons of topography, in small capital letters), without periods between the letters. Unlike acronyms, when an initialism is spoken, each individual letter is pronounced. Example: OAH for the Organization of American Historians.

LAC: the *initialism* (q.v.) used for the Library and Archives Canada, Ottawa.

layered citation: a type of citation needed when a source has been (*a*) processed through multiple media or (*b*) archived in a complex hierarchy, thereby complicating our recital of its description and access information. For archived original documents, separate layers identify each hierarchical level: collection, series, record group, etc. For documents imaged online or on film, separate layers identify (*a*) the imaged record or the extracted data; (*b*) the print, film, or digital publication that provides the image or extracted data; (*c*) the provider's own identification of its source; and (*d*) when needed, comments on the quality of either the source or other relevant issues. Semicolons are used between layers to clearly divide the levels of information.

letterpress copy book: A volume of correspondence created by the letterpress process in which a writer inserts a freshly inked letter into a bound volume of blank tissue pages and, after moistening the adjacent tissue, fastens the closed book with screws; when the book is reopened, the transferred ink can then be read on the tissue that absorbed it. (q.v. *duplicate original*)

liber: the Latin term for *book.* In various jurisdictions, the term has been used for local civil records. Example: a deed register might be referred to as "Deeds, Liber 4."

manuscript: a piece of writing in its native, unpublished state. Derived from the Latin meaning *written by hand,* the term is also applied in modern times to unpublished *typescripts* (q.v.) or other writings that have not been published in print or online.

master source list: a term used by some relational databases to refer to a "pick list" or "master list" of sources identified in an abbreviated form.

minutes: brief notes that describe a proceeding, as in minutes of a court session or a meeting of commissioners. History researchers typically encounter *minutes* as bound volumes created and maintained by a church, a court, or an organization.

monographs: a scholarly piece of writing on a specific (and often narrow) subject, typically book-length.

NARA: the *acronym* (q.v.) used for the U.S. National Archives and Records Administration.

negative argument: A piece of writing that presents all relevant evidence to convincingly rebut a proposed answer to a research question.

negative conclusion: A decision one reaches when all findings convince us that our hypothesis could not possibly be right.

negative evidence: an inference drawn from a silence in the records—from an absence of information or situation that should exist under given circumstances; for validity, the negative must be developed into a positive through additional research and supporting evidence.

negative findings: An outcome occurring when we find sources relevant in some way to our subject, but those sources provide no evidence relevant to our specific research question.

negative search: A failure to find sources or information relevant to our person or subject.

op cit.: Latin abbreviation for *opere citato*, meaning "in the work [of that name, which has already been] cited."

original source: a source that is still in its first recorded or uttered form. The term is also more loosely applied to image copies of an original record when produced by an authoritative or reliable agency—as with microfilm or digital copies produced to preserve the originals or to provide wider access to them.

parenthetical reference: a citation (typically cryptic) placed in parentheses amid a narrative. In its most common form, the author-date system, the parenthetical reference cites just the surname of the author and the year the work was published; the text then concludes with a *bibliography* (q.v.) or *source list* (q.v.) in which all the referenced sources are cited in fuller detail.

plagiarism: the presentation of someone else's words or ideas as one's own, without attribution and appropriate quotation marks—whether copied exactly or paraphrased. An ethical issue not to be confused with the legal issue of *copyright* (q.v.), plagiarism is based on the premise that the ideas and words of others cannot be honorably used without full attribution and permission as needed.

preponderance of the evidence: a legal standard acceptable in civil cases, whereby evidence on one side of an argument outweighs, at least slightly, evidence on the other side of an argument; it is insufficient for historical research.

primary information: statements made or details provided by someone with firsthand knowledge of the facts he or she asserted. Compare to *secondary information* (q.v.).

"primary source": a traditional but vague concept in the humanities that is variously defined as (*a*) an original record, (*b*) a contemporary account, or (*c*) a firsthand account—but not necessarily all three. As a tool for sound historical analysis, it is deficient because any source (and any statement within a source) can be a combination of both firsthand and secondhand knowledge and a mix of both contemporary and recollected information. Compare to *secondary source* (q.v.).

printed primary source: a historic record that has been printed, in full or edited form. It may be an *original record* (q.v.) or a *derivative source* (q.v.), and it may be based on either firsthand knowledge or hearsay, so long as it was created by a person contemporaneous with the times discussed or at least peripherally involved in the incident. Examples: published congressional records, published presidential papers, etc.

proof: a conclusion backed by thorough research, sound analysis, reliable evidence, and a written proof statement or argument.

proof argument: a well-reasoned, meticulously documented piece of writing in which a researcher describes a research problem, the process by which it was solved, and the evidence that supports the conclusion.

proof statement: a sentence or brief statement identifying *direct evidence* (q.v.) that supports an assertion. It may be presented as a *reference note* (q.v.) or it may be woven into our narrative, in which case a *reference note* (q.v.) or notes should fully cite the source or sources invoked.

proof summary: a simple recitation or list of sources that support a conclusion; used when all evidence is direct and no evidence conflicts. When conclusions are based on *indirect evidence* (q.v.) or *conflicting evidence* (q.v.), a *proof argument* (q.v.) is required.

(to) prove: the process of reaching a reliable conclusion through thorough research in quality sources, sound interpretation and correlation of individual pieces of evidence, reliable analysis of the body of evidence, the resolution of *conflicting evidence* (q.v.), and the creation of a *proof argument* (q.v.), *proof statement* (q.v.), or *proof summary* (q.v.) to support the conclusion.

provenance: the origin of a historical object or collection of records; its chain of custody through time.

published source: one that has been distributed in print, online, or via other media; commercial distribution or sale is not required. Compare to *unpublished source* (q.v.).

q.v.: abbreviation for *quod vide* or *quantum vīs,* meaning "which see" or (as used in glossaries) "see this term."

reasonably exhaustive research: the first of the five criteria of the *Genealogical Proof Standard* (q.v.), requiring thorough use of all known records relevant to the research problem and application of all appropriate research methodologies and strategies.

record (noun): an account of an event, circumstance, etc.; a piece of writing created to preserve the memory of certain "facts." Careful researchers do not apply the term to their own *research notes* (q.v.).

record copy: a legal copy of a document, made by an official assigned to create and maintain records. See also *clerk's copy* (q.v.).

reference note: a *citation* (q.v.) or comment placed at the bottom of a page or at the end of a piece of writing and keyed to a particular statement in the text. Its purpose is to identify and/or discuss the source of the specific statement made in the text. See also *footnote* (q.v.) and *endnote* (q.v.).

reliability: *credibility* (q.v.), established by applying sound research and documentation principles.

repository: an archive, government office, library, or other facility where research materials are held.

research: an investigation based on a research question and a research plan, using all appropriate methodology, sources, and strategies to execute the plan. Not to be confused with a basic record search for a specific name, term, event, or object.

research notes: the body of materials accumulated by a historical researcher on a certain subject—including *abstracts, extracts, images, recordings, transcriptions,* and *translations* (q.v., all these terms). Not to be confused with *records* (q.v.).

research plan: a written plan that defines the *research question* (q.v.), states immediate and long-range goals, and identifies the appropriate resources and strategies to be applied. A well-constructed research plan may need ongoing revision as new findings alter the direction in which research should proceed.

research question: the starting point for every research project. It might propose a hypothesis to be proved or disproved. (*Was this* *historic house actually torched by a Confederate fire brigade, rather than the Union army as tradition contends?*) It might define a need to disambiguate between multiple same-name people. (*Do all these records apply to the same man or have two individuals been merged?*) Or it might be as straightforward as *Where was the privateer Jean Lafitte born?*

resolution of conflicting evidence: the process of determining which (if either or any) piece of evidence is likely to be more reliable than another. The process requires (*a*) weighing the strengths and weaknesses of each individual source and the assertion taken from that source; (*b*) playing devil's advocate with one's own reasoning; (*c*) seeking confirmation or disproof in other *independent sources* (q.v.); (*d*) new research in auxiliary resources and/or reconsultation of sources already used; and (*e*) a written explanation of the rationale for discarding some evidence in favor of other contradictory evidence.

secondary information: Details provided by someone with only secondhand knowledge of the facts (q.v. *hearsay*). The term *secondary* is also generically used for *tertiary* (thirdhand) and other levels of knowledge even further removed from the original source.

"secondary source": a traditional but vague term used in the humanities that is variously defined as a copy of a record, an account created long after the fact, or *hearsay* (q.v.). As a tool for sound historical analysis, it fails at its intended task because any source (and any statement within a source) can be a combination of both firsthand and secondhand knowledge. Compare to *primary source* (q.v.).

short-form citation: a sentence-style *citation* (q.v.) that is adopted after a source has been fully identified in a prior *reference note* (q.v.). A short-form citation will typically repeat only the minimum details needed to (*a*) recall and identify the source and (*b*) disambiguate it from any similarly named sources, adding (*c*) specific location data (page, etc.) that supports the new assertion to which the short-form citation is attached. Short-form citations are ill-advised for work-in-progress, given that revisions may eliminate the first full citation to a source.

sic: a Latin term literally translated as *so* or *thus*. Placed in square editorial brackets after a word or phrase that is copied from another source, it is used to inform readers that the text has been copied exactly, even though it may appear to be questionable or erroneous.

site: a location, as in *website*—not to be confused with the words *cite* (as in the act of citing sources) or *sight* (as in *eyesight*).

source: an artifact, book, document, film, person, recording, website, etc., from which information is obtained. Sources are broadly classified as either an *original record* (q.v.), a *derivative source* (q.v.), or an *authored work* (q.v.).

source label: a *citation* (q.v.) appended to a loose document or photocopy, typically constructed in *First Reference Note* (q.v.) format.

source list: a *bibliography* (q.v.) or list of sources used for an essay or a research project; typically but not always arranged in alphabetical order.

source list entry: an individual *citation* (q.v.) within a *source list* (q.v.).

speculation: an opinion untested and unsupported by evidence.

Subsequent Reference Note: an abridged identification of a source that is used to conserve space, once a source has been cited in full in the *First Reference Note* (q.v.). Also see *short-form citation* (q.v.).

supra: a now-archaic Latin term meaning *above*. In source citations, the word follows a shortened title and is used to refer generically to the place in which the full particulars have been given. *Previously cited* is now commonly used in its stead when a notation of that sort is essential.

tertiary information: formally, *thirdhand* information; but in everyday use, the concept of *tertiary information* is usually incorporated into the term *secondary information* (q.v.).

theory: (as used by history researchers) a tentative conclusion drawn after a *hypothesis* (q.v.) has been extensively researched, but the evidence still falls short of standards for *proof* (q.v.).

thesis: a scholarly paper in which one presents findings from his or her investigation of a *hypothesis* (q.v.); also used interchangeably with hypothesis to represent the concept that is being researched.

TNA: the common *initialism* (q.v.) for The National Archives of the United Kingdom.

transcript/transcription: an exact copy of a record, word for word, preserving original punctuation and spelling. Compare to *abstract* (q.v.), *extract* (q.v.), and *translation* (q.v.).

translation: a copy of a source in which the content has been expressed in a different language; not to be confused with *transcription* (q.v.).

typescript: a *manuscript* (q.v.) presented in typed form; or a typed copy of another published or unpublished work.

unpublished source: a source for which only one or a few copies exist; not distributed commercially, and rarely circulated. It may be a *manuscript* (q.v.), a *typescript* (q.v.), a compilation in some other physical form such as a card file, or recorded on some electronic media. Compare to *published source* (q.v.).

verify: to test the accuracy of an assertion by consulting other authoritative and independent sources; a term applied to the process of searching for that independent evidence or the act of finding that independent evidence. Also see *confirm* (q.v.).

vide infra: a Latin phrase that translates as *see below;* once commonly used in scholarly writing but passé today.

vital record: a record of adoption, birth, death, divorce, or marriage.

working source list: a list of sources consulted or to be consulted in a *research* (q.v.) project. A working source list typically contains descriptive or analytical details that will not be published in a final *bibliography* (q.v.), unless the final work intends to present an annotated bibliography. A working source list may also contain references that will not be considered valid or appropriate to the final research product.

Appendix 2: Further Study

GUIDES TO CITATION

ALWD Guide to Legal Citations. Edited by Carolyn V. Williams for the Association of Legal Writing Directors. 7th edition. Los Angeles, California: Aspen Publishing, 2021.

Baker, Donna Cox. *A Quick Guide to Zotero 7: Knowledge Management in Genealogy, History, and Other Fields*. Tuscaloosa, Alabama: Golden Channel Publishing, 2024.

Berlioz, Jacques. *Identifier sources et citations*. Turnhout, Belgium: Brepols, 1994.

The Bluebook: A Uniform System of Citation. Cambridge, Massachusetts: Harvard Law Review Association, frequently revised.

Canadian Guide to Uniform Legal Citation. Edited by *McGill Law Journal*. 9th edition. Toronto: Carswell, 2018. For McGill Style citations.

The Chicago Manual of Style. 18th edition. Chicago: University of Chicago Press, 2024.

Citing Records in the National Archives of the United States. General Information Leaflet no. 17. Washington, D.C.: Government Printing Office. Revised 2010. PDF download. https://www.archives.gov/publications/general-info-leaflets/17-citing-records.html.

Hauptman, Robert. *Documentation: A History and Critique of Attribution, Commentary, Glosses, Marginalia, Notes, Bibliographies, Works-Cited Lists, and Citation Indexing and Analysis*. Jefferson,

Stripped Bare Guide

North Carolina: McFarland, 2008.

Jones, Thomas W. *Mastering Genealogical Documentation*. Arlington, Virginia: National Genealogical Society, 2017.

Lexique des règles typographiques en usage à l'imprimerie nationale. 6th edition. Paris: Imprimerie nationale, 2006.

Lipson, Charles. *Cite Right: A Quick Guide to Citation Styles—MLA, APA, Chicago, the Sciences, Professions, and More.* 3d edition. Chicago: University of Chicago Press, 2018.

McDonald, Ian G. *Referencing for Genealogists: Sources and Citation.* Stroud, Gloucestershire, England: History Press, 2018.

Mills, Elizabeth Shown. *Evidence Explained: Citing History Sources from Artifacts to Cyberspace.* Baltimore: Genealogical Publishing Co., 2024. This volume's 632 pages significantly expand upon *Stripped Bare*, presenting much additional guidance on analysis and citation issues, more-extensive "construction notes" for the templates, and twelve additional chapters exploring many types of records worldwide.

———. *QuickSheet: Citing Ancestry.com Databases and Images, Evidence Style.* Baltimore: Genealogical Publishing Co., 2019.

———. *QuickSheet: Citing Genetic Sources for History Research, Evidence Style.* Baltimore: Genealogical Publishing Co., 2019.

———. *QuickSheet: Citing Online African-American Historical Resources, Evidence Style.* Baltimore: Genealogical Publishing Co., 2010.

———. *QuickSheet: Citing Online Historical Resources, Evidence Style.* Revised edition. Baltimore: Genealogical Publishing Co., 2012.

———. *QuickSheet: Your Stripped-Bare Guide to Citing Sources.* Baltimore: Genealogical Publishing Co., 2014.

MLA Handbook for Writers of Research Papers. 9th edition. New York: Modern Language Association of America, 2021.

OCLC Online Computer Library Center. *WorldCat [Catalog]*. Ongoing updates. https://www.worldcat.org.

Restreto, Irma Isaza. *Citación y descripción de documentos electrónicos.* Medellín, Colombia: Universidad de Antioquia, 2003.

Pérez-Montes, José Enrique. *Manual de citación uniform: un sistema uniforme de Citación para fuentes jurídicas puertorriqueñoas.* 2d ed. San Juan: Escuela de Direcho, Universidad de Puerto Rico, 2024. https://derecho.uprrp.edu/revistajuridica/wp-content/uploads/sites/4/2024/05/FINAL-MCU-2da-Edicion-Edicion-Definitiva-1.pdf. 2024.

Turabian, Kate L. *A Manual for Writers of Research Papers, Theses, and Dissertations: Chicago Style for Students and Researchers.* 9th edition. Revised by Wayne C. Booth, Gregory G. Colomb, et al. Chicago: University of Chicago Press, 2018.

United Kingdom. The National Archives. "Citing Records in The National Archives." Online edition. https://www.nationalarchives.gov.uk/help-with-your-research/citing-records-national-archives/.

United States Congress. "Citation Guide." *Congress.gov.* Undated. https://www.congress.gov/help/citation-guide.

GUIDES TO EVIDENCE ANALYSIS & RESEARCH STRATEGIES

Anderson, Robert Charles. *Elements of Genealogical Analysis.* Boston: New England Historic Genealogical Society, 2014. Kindle edition, 2021.

Best, Arthur. *Evidence: Examples and Explanations.* 14th edition. Los Angeles: Aspen Publishing, 2024.

Board for Certification of Genealogists. *Genealogical Standards.* 2d edition, revised. Nashville and New York: Turner Publishing, Ancestry Imprint, 2021.

Booth, Wayne C.; Gregory G. Colomb; et al. *The Craft of Research.* 5th edition. Chicago: University of Chicago Press, 2024.

Drake, Michael, and Ruth Finnegan, editors. *Sources and Methods for Family and Community Historians: A Handbook.* Vol. 4 of Studying Family and Community History: 19th and 20th Centuries, 2d ed. Cambridge: Cambridge University Press, 1997.

Duranti, Luciana. *Diplomatics: New Uses for an Old Science.* Lanham, Maryland: Scarecrow Press, 1998.

Henige, David. *Historical Evidence and Argument.* Madison: University of Wisconsin Press, 2005.

Jones, Thomas W. *Mastering Genealogical Proof.* Arlington, Virginia: National Genealogical Society, 2013.

Lewis, Jane. *Forensic Document Examination: Fundamentals and Current Trends.* Kidlington, Oxford, England: Academic Press, 2014.

MacNeil, Heather. *Trusting Records: Legal, Historical, and Diplomatic Perspectives.* The Archivist's Library, volume 1. Boston, Massachusetts, and Dordrecht, The Netherlands: Kluwer Academic Publishers, 2010.

Mills, Elizabeth Shown. *QuickSheet: The Historical Biographer's Guide to Cluster Research (the FAN Principle).* Baltimore: Genealogical Publishing Co., 2012.

———. *QuickSheet: The Historical Biographer's Guide to Finding People in Databases & Indexes.* Baltimore: Genealogical Publishing Co., 2012.

———. *QuickSheet: The Historical Biographer's Guide to Individual Problem Analysis—A Strategic Plan.* Baltimore: Genealogical Publishing Co., 2012.

———. *QuickSheet: The Historical Biographer's Guide to the Research Process.* Baltimore: Genealogical Publishing Co., 2012.

———. *QuickSheet: Your Stripped-Bare Guide to Historical 'Proof.'* Baltimore: Genealogical Publishing Co., 2014.

Nickell, Joe. *Detecting Forgery: Forensic Investigation of Documents.* Lexington: University Press of Kentucky, 2005. Kindle edition, 2021.

———. *Pen, Ink, and Evidence: A Study of Writing and Writing Materials for the Penman, Collector, and Document Detective.* New Castle, Delaware: Oak Knoll Press, 2000.

Phelan, Peter J., and Peter J. Reynolds. *Argument and Evidence: Critical Analysis for the Social Sciences.* London and New York: Routledge, 2002.

GUIDES TO STYLE, LEGAL TERMINOLOGY & RELATED MATTERS

Black's Law Dictionary. Bryan A. Garner, editor. 12th edition. Eagen, Minnesota: Thomson Reuters, 2024. History researchers may prefer the 4th edition (St. Paul: West Publishing Co., 1968) for its fuller coverage of terms now obsolete.

Bouvier, John, compiler. *A Law Dictionary: Adapted to the Constitu-tion and Laws of the United States of America and of the Several States of the American Union.* Revised 6th edition, 1856. Online edition. *Constitution Society.* https://constitution.org/1-Consti tution/bouv/bouvier.htm.

Federal Civil Judicial Procedure and Rules. 2024 edition. Eaton, Minnesota: Thomson-West 2024.

Fishman, Stephen. *The Copyright Handbook: What Every Writer Needs to Know.* 15th edition. Berkeley, California: Nolo, 2024.

Harris, Robert A., and Vic Lockman, illustrator. *The Plagiarism Handbook: Strategies for Preventing, Detecting, and Dealing with Plagiarism.* Los Angeles: Pyrczak Publishing, 2001.

Jassin, Lloyd J., and Steven C. Schechter. *The Copyright Permission & Libel Handbook: A Step-by-Step Guide for Writers, Editors, and Publishers.* New York: John Wiley & Sons, 2010.

New Oxford Style Manual. 3d edition, revised. Oxford and New York: Oxford University Press, 2016.

United States. *GPO Style Manual: An Official Guide to the Form and Style of Federal Government Publishing.* Washington, D.C.: Government Printing Office, 2020. Online edition. https://www.govinfo.gov/content/pkg/GPO-STYLEMANUAL-2016/pdf/GPO-STYLEMANUAL-2016.pdf.

*I*ndex ...

A

abbreviation tips, chart of 55
abbreviations and acronyms
    41–42
abstract, defined 107
abstracts
  citing 41
  evaluating 19, 25, 27
access data 72, 80*; also* TEM-
    PLATES 7–8
acronym, defined 41, 107
acronyms, when to use 41–42
administrative copies of records
    26, 31–32
affidavits, evaluating 28, 30, 32
agencies as authors 65; *also* TEM-
    PLATES 8, 9, 10
agreement between records 33
analysis, defined 107
analysis
  importance of 9–10, 23
  reliability, achieving 33, 34
archives, formal
  factors to consider when citing
    75, 80; *also* TEMPLATE 8
artifacts, citing 68; *also* TEMPLATE
    7
artificial intelligence tools and
    websites 85, 89, TEMPLATE 5

assertion, defined 107
attention to details 36, 51
attested copy, defined 107
authenticity, evaluating 31
authors and creators
  agencies as authors 65–66; *also*
    TEMPLATES 8, 14
  anonymous authors 65
  authors of letters. TEMPLATE 7
  churches as authors. TEMPLATE 9
  citation block for 65–66
  evaluating reliability of 28, 29
  government offices as authors
    65–66; *also* TEMPLATES 8, 9, 10
  multiple authors 65
  role of authors, specifying 65
authored manuscript, citing. TEM-
    PLATE 6
authored work, defined 108

B

basic citation formats
  for publications 79
  for unpublished works 79–80
best evidence, defined 108
"Best Evidence Rule" 25

"beyond reasonable doubt," legal standard, defined 22, 108
Bible entries, evaluating 29, 30, 32
bibliographies
  alphabetizing 57
  compiling 57
  formatting 56, 84
  guidelines for 25
  numbering of 57
  punctuation within 84
  purpose of 40
  subdividing 57
bibliography, defined 40, 108
birth certificates. *See* artifacts *and* vital records
brackets
  angle, use of 56
  square (editorial), use of 56, 86
building a case 23–24
building blocks for citations 62, 64, 65–73

C

calendar (archival context), defined 108
capitalization issues 52–53, 56, 67, 68
case building 23–24
"case closed," false concept 18, 34
censuses
  citing 45, 100; *also* TEMPLATE 13
  evaluating reliability of 17, 19
certificates, as evidence 27
certified copies, as evidence 27
cf. and other Latin terms used in citations 52
charts, citations for 36, 46–47
circumstantial case, defined 108
circumstantial evidence, defined 108
citation, art rather than science 11
citation, building blocks for 62, 64, 65–73
  assembling the blocks 79–81

citation, building blocks for (cont.)
  Block 1: Creator (*who?* question) 65–66
  Block 2: Title (*what?* question) 66
  Block 3: Descriptor (*what?* question) 66–67, 72
  Block 4: Place (*where?* question) 67–70
  Block 5: Publisher (*who?* question) 70–71
  Block 6: Date/Year (*when?* question) 71–72
  Block 7: Specific Item (*where?* and *where within?* questions) 72–73
citation, defined 108
citation sentence, defined 108
citations, guidelines for
as self-help 35
best possible source, importance of 37
building blocks of 62–73
clear citations 36, 51–54
complexity of historical citations 61
construction of 61–80
ethical issues 48–49
endnotes vs. footnotes 42–43
five questions every citation must answer 62
footnotes vs. endnotes 42–43
full citations, when to use 40–41, 47
history/humanities style vs. scientific style 43
hypertext 43
layers. *See* layered citations
legal issues 48–49
parenthetical citations 43
purposes or goals of 11, 35, 36, 37, 38
scientific style vs. humanities/ history style 43
shortened citations, cautions and when to use 40–41

citations, guidelines for (cont.)
  structure of 80
  types used for history research 62
  when to use 36, 37–38
cite, defined 109
Cite Your Sources, manual 9–10
citing, by type or detail
  access details 75–76
  addresses. TEMPLATES 7, 14
  agency records 80
  archival collections 75, 80
  archival files 75
  archival labels 80
  archival record groups 75
  archival series 75
  archived manuscripts 73–74, 75,
    77; *also* TEMPLATE 8
  ARKs vs. URLs 69
  articles in periodicals 56
  artifacts 68; *also* TEMPLATE 7
  authored manuscripts 77; *also*
    TEMPLATE 6
  blogs 70, 72, 73
  book covers, caution 51
  books 51, 67, 70, 72; *also* TEM-
    PLATE 1
  CD-ROMs and CD-DVDs 70
  cemeteries 74
  censuses 45; *also* TEMPLATE 13
  chapters in books 5; *also* TEM-
    PLATE 2
  church records. TEMPLATES 9, 11
  collections. TEMPLATE 8
  column numbers 73, 86
  courthouse "loose files" or record
    books. TEMPLATE 9
  databases 67, 76–78; *also* TEM-
    PLATES 1, 5, 10, 13
  dates 71–72
  death certificates. *See* artifacts
    and vital records
  derivative works 48
  diaries 45, 67
  dissertations, theses. TEMPLATE 6
  documents 66–67, 71, 73,
    75–77; *also* TEMPLATES 8, 9

citing, by type or detail (cont.)
  editions 66
  editors, citing. TEMPLATE 2
  family papers. TEMPLATE 7
  family trees 67
  figure numbers 72, 73
  file folders. TEMPLATE 8
  files with multiple documents 73
  frame numbers vs. page numbers
    78
  government records. TEMPLATE 9
    See also agency records *and spe-*
      cific record types
  gravestones 74; *also* TEMPLATE 14
  image group numbers. TEMPLATE
    10
  images, online 76–78; *also* TEM-
    PLATE 10
  journal articles 66, 70, 72, 73;
    also Template 3
  journals, personal 67
  layered citations 51, 62, 73–79;
    also TEMPLATES 5–13
  legal records 45
  letters 67; *also* TEMPLATE 7
  magazine articles 70, 72; *also*
    TEMPLATE 3
  manuscript titles 93
  manuscripts 54, 56, 68, 70, 71,
    75, 77; *also* TEMPLATES 5, 6, 8
  maps 67, 70
  marriage registers 70
  microfilm, preservation copy. TEM-
    PLATES 11, 13
  multiple sources in one note 44,
    74
  multiple sources in same citation
    sentence, caution 75
  multivolume works 67, 72
  newspaper articles 56, 70, 72, 73;
    also TEMPLATE 4
  one-of-a-kind items 68
  online access 76
  original records 48, 71, 73, 75
    online images of 76–78; *also*
      TEMPLATE 10

citing, by type or detail (cont.)
  page numbers 72, 73, 78
  page numbers vs. frame numbers
    78
  PALs vs. URLs 69
  paths 69–70; *also* TEMPLATES
    10, 11
  periodicals 67; *also* TEMPLATE 3
  place of access 68
  place of creation 67
  place of publication 67
  postnominals 56
  privately held items 80
  probate records. TEMPLATE 10
  publication date 71
  publications, basic format 79
  publishers 70
  section names 73
  series, citing 67
  source of our source 48
  source statements separated
    from personal opinion 44–46
  specific item in books, at web-
    sites, etc. 72
  spines of books, caution 51
  tax rolls. TEMPLATE 8
  theses 90; *also* TEMPLATE 6
  titles 51, 63–64
  undated items 71
  vital records. TEMPLATE 12 (*see
    also* artifacts)
  volume numbers 72
  waypoints 69–70; *also* TEM-
    PLATES 10, 11
  websites, web pages, and other
    items 67, 68, 70, 72, 73, 103;
    also TEMPLATES 1, 5, 10, 13
claim, defined 109
"*clear and convincing evidence,*" le-
    gal standard, defined 22, 109
clerical notes in record books 28
clerk's copy, defined 109
"common knowledge," determining
    36–38
compendiums, as evidence 27
compiled work, defined 109

conclusion, defined 109
conclusions
  basis for 18
  case never closed 18, 34
  reliability of 35
confirm, defined 109
conflict resolution and standards
    for 23, 46–47
conflicting evidence, defined 109
conflicts in information or evidence
    11, 16, 21
contemporaneousness,
    evaluating 18, 30, 32
content of citations
  input vs. *output* 11
context, importance of 20
contradictions between sources
    11, 16, 21
copying from others 48–49
copyright, avoiding problems with
    49–50
copyright, defined 109
corrections 26, 48, 53
correlation, defined 109
correlation, importance of 10, 23
corroborate, defined 109
court cases, reliability of 19
creators, skill and veracity of 18
credibility, defined 34
credibility, evaluating 34
credit, when to give 48–49
critical examination, importance
    of 16
cross-references within notes 42
custodial history of records 18,
    32–33

D

damage claims, evaluating 28
database, defined 27
databases and database entries
  citing 67, 76–78, 85
  database as website. TEMPLATE 1
  database at complex website.
    TEMPLATE 5

databases and database entries (cont.)
  evaluating reliability of 25, 27
  titles of 67, 78
data sheets, citations on 36,
    46–47
dates
  access dates (online) 72, 80; *also*
    TEMPLATES 9, 10, 13
  access dates (physical). TEM-
    PLATES 8, 14
  creation dates 71–72
  evaluating 29, 31
  guidelines for citing 71–72
  missing dates 71; *also* TEMPLATE
    8
  revision dates 72
death certificates
  evaluating 29 (*see also* artifacts
    and vital records)
deduction, defined 110
deed books
  as evidence 28
  citing. TEMPLATE 9
"definitive source," defined 110
derivative materials
  attested copy, defined 107
  certificates 27
  clerk's copy, defined 109
  examined copy, defined 111
  exhibition copy, defined 111
  form-style books 32
  reliability 18, 24, 26–28
  tracking ancestry of derivatives
    28
  types of derivatives 26–27
  using derivatives 48–49
  vs. original records 18
derivative source, defined 110
details, importance of 36, 51
diaries
  as evidence 17, 26
  citing 45
  evaluating 29
direct evidence, defined 110. *See
    also* evidence
discursive note, defined 110

document, defined 110
document label, defined 110
document labels, format for 63
documentation
  "common knowledge" rule 36
  purpose of 36
  soundness of 23
duplicate, defined 25
duplicate original, defined 110
duplicates
  admissibility of 25–26
  reliability of 25

E

edition, defined 110
editors, citing role of 65
ellipses, use of 56
em dashes, use of 57
endnote, defined 43, 111
endnotes, advantages and when to
    use 43
errors
  in derivative works 16, 21, 48–49
  in original documents 16, 21
ethical issues, when citing sources
    36, 48–49
evidence, defined 20, 111
evidence issues
  "Best Evidence Rule" 25
  "beyond a reasonable doubt" 22
  body of, as basis for proof 24
  circumstantial, defined 108
  "clear and convincing" 22
  direct evidence, defined 20
    case building with 21
    reliability of 20
  evidence books, defined 111
  indirect evidence, defined 20
  indirect evidence, use of
    case building 20–21
    weighing 20
  legal terms used for 22
  negative evidence
    as silence in the records 20
    vs. negative findings 20

Stripped Bare Guide

evidence issues (cont.)
  vs. negative search 20
  "preponderance of the evidence"
    22
  quality vs. quantity 21
  quantity vs. weight 18
  vs. information 17–18
  vs. proof 17–18
  vs. sources 17–18
  weighing evidence 22
  weight vs. quantity 18, 20, 21
*Evidence! Citation & Analysis for
  the Family Historian* 10
*Evidence Explained: Citing His-
  tory Sources from Artifacts to
  Cyberspace* 10
Evidence Style citations 11, 44,
  69, 74–75
examined copy, defined 111
exhibition copy, defined 111
extract, defined 27, 111
extracts, evaluating 19, 27

F

facsimile, defined 111
fact, defined 16–17, 111
factoid, defined 111
"facts" 16–17
  "definitive" facts 34
"fair copy," defined 111
Fair Use Doctrine, defined 111
  application of 49–50
*Federal Civil Judicial Procedure and
  Rules* 25–26
firsthand knowledge 18
First Reference Note, defined 112
Five Ws of citation 37, 38, 62,
  63–64
folio, defined 112
font issues 52–53, 56
footnote, defined 42, 112
footnotes,
  advantages of 42–43
  when to use 42–43

forgeries 32
fraud, guarding against 32
FamilySearch, citing. TEMPLATES
  10, 11
FSL (initialism), defined 112

G

Genealogical Proof Standard 23
Genealogical Proof Standard (GPS),
  defined 112
genealogy, defined 112
government records
  citing. TEMPLATES 8, 9, 10, 11
  evaluating 29–30
gravestones
  citing online data 103
  citing stone personally visited.
    TEMPLATE 14
Guidelines for Analyzing Evidence
  (fig. 1) 18
Guidelines for Documentation (fig.
  2) 36

H

hearsay, defined 112
hearsay, using 29
hypertext, advantages vs. problems
  43
hypothesis, defined 112

I

ibid., defined 112
ibid., when and how to use 52
identity
  clues to 31
  conclusions about 34
  signatures or marks 31
image copy, defined 113
imaged records 25
  as cause of complex citations 61
  citations affixed to 63
  electronic but not online 54

imaged records (cont.)
  layered citations for 76–78
  published vs. unpublished 54
independent source, defined 113
independently created sources, us-
    ing 24–25
indexes, reliability issues 25
indirect evidence, defined 113.
    See also evidence
"indirect source," defined 113
inference, defined 113
informants, reliability of 18, 29
information
  critical analysis of 16
  errors and false leads 15, 37
  origin or provenance 24
  primary, defined 19, 115
  questions to be answered 15
  secondary, defined 19, 118
  vs. evidence 17–18
  vs. proof 17–18
  vs. source 17–18
  vs. truth 15
information, defined 113
infra and other Latin terms 52
initialism, defined 113
initialisms, using 41–42
input vs. *output* (citation content)
    11
italics, use of 52, 56

K

knowledge
  "common knowledge" rule 36–38
  firsthand vs. secondhand 18, 29

L

Lackey, Richard S. 9–10
Latinisms, use of 52
layered citation, defined 113–14
layered citations
  access layer 76
  cautions when using 51
  "citing ..." layer 76

layered citations (cont.)
  emphasis on database 78; *also*
    TEMPLATE 5
  emphasis on record 77
  flexibility of 73
  for archived manuscripts 73, 80
  for artifacts. TEMPLATE 7
  for authored manuscripts. TEM-
    PLATE 6
  for blogs 74
  for books 75
  for courthouse "loose files." TEM-
    PLATE 9
  for courthouse record books.
    TEMPLATES 9, 10
  for databases 76, 78; *also* TEM-
    PLATES 1, 5
  for journal articles. TEMPLATE 3
  for maps 74
  for newspaper items. TEMPLATE 4
  for online images 76; *also* TEM-
    PLATE 10
  for preservation microfilm. TEM-
    PLATES 11, 13
  for print publications 74
  for websites 74; *also* TEMPLATES
    5, 10, 13
  for wills, probates. TEMPLATE 10
  guidelines to apply 51, 62
  interchangeability of 51
  location layer 76, 90
  provenance layer, citing. TEM-
    PLATES 7, 12
  record layer 76, 90
  sequence of layers 77–78
  single-layer citations 74
  when needed 51, 73–74
legal issues when citing sources
    36, 48–49
legal records, evaluating 28, 32–33
letterpress copy book, defined 114
letterpress process 26
letters
  citing. TEMPLATE 7
  evaluating 32
liber, defined 114

Library of Congress, online catalog 51
local record abstracts, citing 41
loose papers, published vs. unpublished 54

M

manuscript, defined 114
manuscripts
  citing. TEMPLATES 6–12
  published vs. unpublished 53–54
  titles of 56
  undated 71
marriage records, evaluating 32
master source list, defined 114
memoirs and diaries
  as evidence 17, 26
  citing 45
  evaluating 29
microfilm sources
  as preservation copies 54; *also*
    TEMPLATE 10
  as publications 54
minutes (court records), defined 114
monographs, defined 114

N

names
  agencies as authors 93
  of authors 57, 84
  of persons of interest 93
  of series 67
NARA, acronym for U.S. National
    Archives 114
narrative account, defined 19, 27
narrative accounts, as evidence 27
negative argument, defined 114
negative conclusion, defined 114
negative evidence, defined 115
negative evidence, using 20
negative findings, defined 20, 115
negative search, defined 20, 115
newspapers 17; *also* TEMPLATE 4
notetaking practices 63

number of sources for proof 20, 21, 34
numbering
  of columns 78, 86
  of frame numbers 78
  of notes 44–46
  of pages 72, 73, 78
  of source lists 44–46
  of volumes 72
numbers for online image groups,
    citing. TEMPLATE 10
nutshells, as evidence 27

O

online sources, special citation issues 36, 50–51
op. cit., defined 115
op. cit., using 52
oral history, as evidence 27
organization of archives, as citation
    issue 75
organization of websites, as citation issue 77–79
origin, conclusions about 34
original source, defined 115
original sources 17, 18, 19, 25, 71
originals vs. derivatives, evaluating
    17, 18, 19, 31–32

P

page numbers 72, 73, 78
  vs. frame numbers 78
parentage, conclusions about 34
parenthetical reference, defined 115
parenthetical references, using 36
paths, citing 69–70; *also* TEMPLATES 10, 11
penmanship
  ancestral 31
  evaluating 18, 30–31
  scribal 31–32
pension affidavits, evaluating 28, 30
permissions from others 49–50

plagiarism, defined 115
plagiarism, how to avoid 49–50
postnominals 56
preponderance of the evidence,
   legal standard, defined 22,
   115
presidential papers, as evidence
   26
primary information, defined 115
"primary source," defined 17,
   115–16
printed primary source, defined
   116
proof
   achieving 17–18, 21, 24
   number of sources needed 24–25
   proof arguments 23
   proof statements 23
   proof summaries 23
   proof vs. evidence 17–18
   proof vs. information 17–18
proof, defined 116
proof argument, defined 116
proof statement, defined 116
proof summary, defined 116
(to) prove, defined 116
provenance, defined 116
provenance issues
   citing 91; *also* TEMPLATE 7
   evaluating 32
publication dates 30, 32, 71–72, 80
published vs. unpublished sources
   definitions of each 53–54,
   116–17, 20
   differences in formatting titles of
   each type 53–54
published source, defined 116
publishers, citing 70
punctuation
   correction of 26
   for bibliographies 57, 84
   for citing archived documents 81
   within titles 53
   within URLs 68–69
purpose of records, evaluating
   28–29

Q

quotation marks
   use of 27, 48, 49, 56, 66, 79
   vs. italics 56, 66, 79
quotations
   ethical issues 36, 49–50
   guidelines for using 49

R

reasonably exhaustive research,
   defined 117
record (noun), defined 116
record copy, defined 117
records and sources
   custodial history 18
   derivative, defined 19, 110
   imaged online 36, 50–51
   motivation for 18
   narrative accounts vs. records
   19
   original, defined 19, 115
   original vs. derivative 18
   processing, effect on reliability 28
   provenance 18
   purpose of 18
   reliability of 9, 18, 28–29
   self-serving nature 28
   timeliness of 18
reference note, defined 117
   See also source notes
reliability, defined 117
reliability of researchers 24, 33
repository, citing. TEMPLATES 6–9,
   10, 12
repository, defined
research, defined 9–10, 117
research, standards for
   core challenge 15, 16–17
   importance of standards 16
   methods and strategies 16
   reasonably exhaustive, as a standard 22
   reliability 21
   thoroughness of 18, 21, 22, 24

Stripped Bare Guide

research notes, defined 117
research plan, defined 117
research question, defined 117
research reports, documentation
    for 47
resolution of conflicting evidence,
    defined 117
resolution of conflicting evidence,
    standards for 23, 46–47

S

scribes, evaluating 29–30
secondary information, defined 118
    See also information
"secondary source," defined 118
short-form citation, defined 118
signatures 31–32
skill of creator, assessing 28–29
sic, defined 118–19
site, defined 119
source, defined 119
source label, defined 119
source list, defined 119
source list entry, defined 119
source lists. *See* bibliographies
source notes
  bibliographic 36
  endnotes 36
  ethical issues 36, 48
  footnotes 36, 42–43
  for data sheets 36
  for document copies 36, 47
  for family charts 46–47
  for narrative accounts 36, 42–43
  for research reports 47
  formats, basic 36, 40
  full notes vs. shortened notes 36,
    40–41
  full notes, when to use 47, 62
  full reference note as default for
    history research 62
  functions of 39
  how tracked 40
  hypertext, use of 36
  legal issues 36

source notes (cont.)
  numbering of 44–46
  parenthetical citations 36
  purposes of 36, 38, 39, 40
  risky practices 40–42
  separating source statements
    from interpretations and con-
    clusions 44–46
  shortened citations
    best practices for 41
    risks of 40–42
    when to use 62
  superscript, use of 44–45
  value of 37
  when to use 40
  where to place 44–46
sources, using
  are not created equal 10
  as containers of information 17,
    19
  "borrowing," caution 48
  credibility of 20–21
  evaluation of 19, 35
  "gold standard," citing 48
  how tracked 40
  independently created 24
  nature of 24
  number of sources for proof
    20–21, 34
  numbering of 44–46
  original, reliability of 25
  original vs. derivative records 17,
    18, 19
  "primary vs. secondary" 17
  provenance of 32, 91, 116
  quality of 24
  self-serving nature 28
  sources vs. evidence 17–18
  sources vs. information 17–18
  sources vs. proof 17–18
  "trustworthy" sources 24
  unpublished 53–54, 81, 120
speculation, defined 119
stylistic issues 52, 56
subsequent reference note, defined
    119

successful research, defined 9
superscript numbers
  for generations 44–45·
  for sources 44–45
supra, defined 119
  use of 52

T

technology and fraud 32
templates
  designed for flexibility 83
  examples, not rigid formulas 83

  for publications
  1: Basic Publication
    • Book 84
    • Simple Website 85
  2: Book with Parts by Different
     Authors 86
  3: Journal or Magazine Article 87
  4: Newspaper Article 88
  5: Complex Website (Multiple
     Articles or Databases) 89

  for unpublished materials
  6: Basic Authored Manuscript 90
  7: Private Holdings (Artifact or
     Manuscript Document) 91
  8: Formal Archives (Artifact or
     Manuscript Document) 92–93
  9: Government, Church, or Cor-
     porate Office
    • Record Book 94
    • Loose File 95
  10. Online Image, in
    • Named Database 96
    • No Named Database 97
  11. Preservation Microfilm 98

  for miscellaneous materials
  12. Birth or Death Certificate (Not
      a Family Artifact) 99
  13. Census
    • Online Image 100
    • Preservation Film 101
  14. Gravestone (Used Personally)
      102–3

tertiary information, defined 119
theory, defined 119
thesis, citing. TEMPLATE 6
thesis, defined 119
  See also hypothesis
thoroughness, need for 18, 21, 22,
     24, 33, 37
timeliness of records 18, 30
title block in citations
  guidelines for 66
titles
  as descriptor for content 64
  capitalization of 52–53, 66, 68
  collection titles 93
  correcting errors in 53
  eponymous titles 66
  errors within 53
  folder titles 93
  font issues with 52–53
  italics vs. quotation marks
     53–54, 66
  language differences 53
  manuscript titles 56
  punctuation issues 53
  untitled works 66
tombstones, gravestones
  citing online data 103
  citing stone personally visited.
     TEMPLATE 14
TNA, initialism for The National
     Archives, United Kingdom
     120
tradition 112
transcript, transcription, defined
     120
transcripts, transcriptions, use of
  edited 26
  errors in 28
  evaluating 19, 25, 26, 28
translations, evaluating 19, 25
translators, identification of role
     65
trust 16, 24, 26, 32, 34
"truth" 16, 38
typescript, defined 120

Stripped Bare Guide

U

undated manuscripts 71
understanding sources, importance
   of 9, 11
unpublished source, defined 53–
   54, 120
unpublished sources, using
  basic format for citing 81
  differences in handling titles
    53–54
unpublished vs. published sources
   54
untitled works 66
URLs (Uniform Resource Locators)
  ARKs (Archival Resource Keys) 69
  case sensitivity 68
  citing 66
  dynamic URLs, caution 68
  line breaks within 69
  long URLs 68–69
  PALs (Paradox Applications Lan-
    guage) 68
  paths, citing 68–70; *also* TEM-
    PLATES 10, 13
  punctuation within 68–69
  waypoints, citing 69–70; *also*
    TEMPLATES 10, 13
U.S. Code, Fair Use Doctrine 50

V

van der Rohe, Mies, quoted 51
Velcro Principle for layered citations 78
veracity, evaluating 18, 63
verify, defined 120
vide infra, defined 120
vital record, defined 120
vital records, citing. TEMPLATE 14

W

Wallace, Lew 30
waypoints, citing 69–70; *also* Templates 10, 13
websites
  as publications 85
  capitalization of titles 58
  citing complex website. TEM-
    PLATE 5
  citing, general rules for 68
  citing simple website. TEMPLATE 1
  eponymous sites 66
  layered citations, use of 74
  paths and waypoints, use of
    69–70; also TEMPLATES 10, 13
  same citation format as books 85
  using descriptor blocks for 67
wills
  citing. TEMPLATE 10
  evaluating 32
working source list, defined 120
WorldCat, online catalog 52
writing styles, evaluating 31
wrong information, handling of 37,
   39

138

Elizabeth Shown Mills

Mills is a historical writer with decades of research experience in public and private records of many Western nations. Across a half-century, her books, book chapters, and essays on historical topics have been published by six university presses; and her dozens of peer-reviewed articles have appeared in journals within the fields of history, genealogy, sociology, and literature. Her text books and reference works have become classic guides for history researchers.

Amid those writings, Mills edited a national-level scholarly journal for sixteen years, taught for thirteen years at a National Archives–based institute on archival records and, for twenty-eight years, headed a university-based program in advanced research methodology.

Mills knows records, loves records, and regularly shares her expertise in using them with live and media audiences around the globe. This latest work, she hopes, will ease your own labors as you explore the past and share your findings with others curious about the people and events that created our present world.

www.ingramcontent.com/pod-product-compliance
Lightning Source LLC
Chambersburg PA
CBHW061749270326
41928CB00011B/2437